A STATE OF MIND

written by
Dillon M. Jepsen

Dillon Jepsen
Florida, United States
www.dillonjepsen.com

Publisher's Note: This is a work of creative non-fiction. Names, characters, places, and incidents are anecdotes from the Author's life.

Book Cover Art by Adam Varga
Editing by Patricia Scott

A STATE OF MIND/ Dillon Jepsen. -- 1st ed.
ISBN: 9781982913472

If you enjoyed the book, leave a review! It is appreciated.

Special thanks to,

My family loved ones and close friends for supporting
me throughout some of the roughest parts of my life.
Thank you for always listening to me and thank you
for giving me the right amount of space to grow and
become all that I can be.

Heaven is a STATE OF MIND. Hell is a STATE OF MIND.
Your ETERNITY is within the confines OF THIS MIND.
Alter this STATE and go BEYOND MIND into SPIRIT.

—A STATE OF MIND

CONTENTS

CHAPTER ONE

DEEP INTO THE ABYSS

What is the Abyss? It is the unreachable depths of your imagination. It is entirely personal. The scope of this place is determined by your interest in knowing and finding out more. Fears and blessings are hidden within this arena of thought. The way you choose to envision, understand, and know it is all relative to how much capacity you allow it to have.

Who am I? I will go by Mark. I am an old man... twenty-something years is a long time. Well, enough time to at least capture this much content in this writing. I am a happy guy. I enjoy living life to its highest potential. Through the progressing of this text, I have experienced plenty of self-development. I will try to keep my beliefs consistent. Mind you, if you are standing still looking at the same problems, they will consume you. Instead, press forward, allowing your retrospective 'higher self' to correct the errors when you meet those moments and learn those lessons.

Have you ever encountered someone who pursues an attitude or agenda that is obstructive to rationality? I hate that … it is like an evangelical telling me that believing in a dead person may grant me eternal life. That was supposed to humor you, the reader. If it did not, I am guessing you are onto something … something cluing you into a fond relationship with higher reality, onto a journey that is leading you into harmony and communion with God.

Though, what if you let yourself have a chuckle? That is great … I find much humility in feeling like life is a big joke too. But guess what? Life is not a joke. It is very serious, profound, and incredible. What if you went to Hell, after all the time of you denying the plausible nature of an occurring afterlife that exists entirely independent to your mind? Would that not be quite dreadful? I ponder these thoughts for those who do not believe.

Calloused by disbelief and an atheism that at times could be rather cold-hearted. I possessed confidence in the 'truth' of there being no afterlife. Let me explain something very clearly to you as the reader. I will never convince you; I will only guide you through my mind – within your reading experience. I know you can muster some sort of wherewithal to perceive this narrative within your mind's eye. Keep this understanding and practice within you, for the duration of your reading. It is all worth the effort, you will see why in later chapters.

The creative brain can read into the literary text, fabricating an interpretation or images from the descriptive texts we perceive. The result is your reproduction of the story within the conscious mind. Think back to previous books you have read, to the impact they left on your limitless and impressionable mind?

It begins, yes, I have started a procession of thoughts. The sum of those ideas will walk down a red carpet laid throughout the hallway of your mind into an opening where your feminine and masculine spirit will be engaged in unity. This unifying experience will move (or sail) forth into your spirit, and your imagination by the end of this book will possess logic, reasoning, and God.

. . .

I was eighteen years old when I began facing nihilistic tendencies of existentialism. Within my private introversion, I was searching upon philosophy and physics at the time, and a little religion. Yes, in this mode of my life, I had a creeping anxiousness residing in me, the desire to understand the unknown becoming more undeniable. I wanted to know more because I knew I could know more. I spent that year delving into basic concepts of the living universe, as well as exploring the internet for deep thinkers and scholars to identify with. I found none at the time that compelled me to look inside myself.

I encountered a 'state of mind' unlike any other mindset during this age of young adulthood. My boyfriend at the time soothed my ego-centric being into harmony with my existence. Our love expressed even in small, seemingly insignificant moments, granted added significance to every moment. At the time, I was taking my first sociology course and a religious studies introductory course. I spent time putting forth the effort to understand the wisdom of Eckhart Tolle. I connected and intertwined the Freudian mind (the id, ego, and super-ego) with my emotional and passive identity.

I made love to my boyfriend by painting my childlike spirit and character onto him with every kiss, motion, and touch. We became synchronized with a connection of heart and mind. The timing of every kiss was so synchronized with the mind that it was impeccable. This was a part of my early stages of energy-work. Discussing this with him, after the relationship, he accounted the bliss we felt to a level of comfort we experienced with each other. I cannot deny that I was very comfortable in his presence. The stress of everyday life seemed to melt away when we spent time together. We dated for three months and held onto the relationship for a little over a year, and now we are good friends.

Towards the end of 2011, my father went through traumatic experiences with mental illness. I went to visit him and counter his suicidal thoughts. I explained to him to the best of my ability on how he might calm his racing mind. His mind was reevaluating life amid a crisis of spirit. The rain poured from the sky, creating an ambient landscape of calming sounds that filled every direction in all nearby spaces within the surrounding distance. I expressed the thoughts of my young mind to my father ... harmonies, sounds, and frequencies can be used as a blanket to cover the spirit with comforting stimulus.

Rain helps soothe an erratic mind and helps a person sober towards reality – grounding them to a stillness within the physical world. In finding the added purpose and significance of every moment you experience; you may mature the soul by finding the necessary and critical practices of self-development. Receiving your higher identity to bind to your psyche motivates your spirit when preparing. Preparing for what? ... Preparation for transcending the ego, and eventually when the time is right, ascending beyond this lower realm of chaos.

> *"The road to creativity passes so close to the madhouse and often detours or ends there."*
>
> *Ernest Becker*

When the world was prophesied to end in 2012, I had a psychotic episode on the days around January 23rd. I was awake for over eighty hours without any legitimate rest. I began to hallucinate, deluding myself with irrational thoughts while uncontrollably pacing from room to room in my house. While standing in front of the bathroom mirror, I observed my reflection, my eyes started dilating, and no, I was not on any mood-altering or chemistry-changing psychedelics or drugs.

However, while in that moment my mind reached for any plausible explanation for what was happening to me. My conscience told me I was *biologically awakening* and heightened in my senses. I had always perceived since then, that when the pupils become magnified, that the spirit was simply coming from within consciousness for a closer look.

"Fluoride, there must be fluoride that is killing me in my toothpaste" thought my frantic mind. My mind began to wander hysterically, as it started to infer that there were toxic ingredients in our food, and even our drinking water. I would not have been able to tell you if the poisoning was intentional with the knowledge I had back then. However, these days I have an opinion. I would be quick to state that hastening death of masses would be a corrupted elitist strategy to prevent an intellectually rooted uprising. Simply put, in theory, poison the working-class to stunt rises in class-consciousness. Through adding toxins to their bodies, you can depreciate the progress of their brain development.

I laid on the couch until I was called to the door. I was in an altered state of mind while having lunch with my mother, or you could say "perma-trip".

I was brought to a hospital, where doctors found nothing wrong with me. All I can recall from laying in the hospital bed, is them repeatedly telling me to sleep which I perceived as coded language for "just die already" in my mind. I was intrigued by my psychological state, causing me to look deeper into my mind. The further my consciousness alienated from reality, the more I began to perceive thoughts that I could not claim as my own. As I was being pushed around in a wheelchair around the county hospital rather aimlessly, I started invading the minds of the nurses, social workers, and hospital staff. I tried to rationalize what was happening. You could say that the irrational hemisphere of my brain took the initiative to make sense of things ...

"Perhaps I'm psychic, and they are keeping quiet about what's going on," thought my observing mind, directing myself to accept this was not a regular visit to the emergency room. It surely was not.

I unknowingly received transportation from the hospital to an inpatient mental ward. While being escorted and sitting in the backseat of a car with the middle of the interior separated by thick plastic, I thought to myself, "I am getting a personal taxi to the federal government, to a top-secret location where psychics are processed."

I entered the mental ward and was taken through processing. Signing papers giving proper consent while in a mental institution and being entirely unaware that you are getting admitted is not easy when you are mentally unstable with no prior experience of ever being mentally ill. This seems like *Alice in Wonderland* type of shit, right?

In some ways, you may relate it to that narrative. Except this is not a story, it is your life. Narrated by the little voice in your head, the conscience of yourself. What do you think Hell is a place of fiction an alternate reality, or is it all in your mind? I will tell you; it is all in your mind. It is not a work of fiction, for it is made of the same 'substance' as what you may identify as the impressions left on your passive mind from the sensory of previous lived experiences.

I remember Hell like it was yesterday, but I did not have to pass through a physical death to enlighten you during my journey through Hell. I was only there periodically, for I went up and down the planes by a revealed fate as directed by the Most High God. I spent all of 2012 soul traveling through gateways of perception that may be simply understood as 'planes of mind'. These planes reside as the foundation of physical reality. They are within the capacity of our collective mind and may be accessed through our minds.

In the mental ward, my parents were saying goodbye to me as I sat inside an isolated square room. They talked to me as if I were never going to be sane again. I was lost, and I knew I was going to be lost for several months. Time slowly slid into the night;

Looking up at the television, I noticed it was doing exactly as my mind directed, I thought "how in the fuck?" In shock I stood up in the common room during the after-hours of an incredibly dead environment. I picked up a nearby chair and smashed the television, shattering it.

A TV that once was spitting the image of a horror flick, now appeared less of a threat to me in its broken form. Horror is not what you want on television when you are providing entertainment for the mentally ill. I held the disposition that the movie was not staged, and that it may have been an instance occurring in real-life. I was aggressive in my reaction because I held the attitude that the unsuspecting victim should not have to die at the hands of a devious murderer.

I collapsed onto the floor with every force counteracting gravity that held my being dissipating as my strength escaped. I immediately shut my eyes, attempting to pass onto another plane of mental dimension once more. I was aware of the reality I was locked in this room with nowhere to go. I knew this, as I had already attempted to escape. I faced opposition from the hospital staff who resisted my attempts to escape by pulling my fingers off the door handle. I had an incentive to go outside into the wild. I had a real burning desire to go on the journey of maturation that every Native American took when they go on a vision quest to experience altered states of consciousness.

Isn't it interesting that my newly schizophrenic ass wanted to go on a vision quest like all awakening shamans, by pure instinct? Nope motherfucker, this is America and here we do not do that. I was pulled by two unidentified hands, and my inanimate and lifeless body was dragged a few directions, then was let go near a bed in a very small room. A slightly overweight man sat on a chair outside my small safe space, he sat there for hours and monitored my emotional well-being. I was informed in those moments by a voice or thought from God. That as a non-believer, I was to go to Hell.

Gnosticism teaches that salvation occurs when exercising the willpower of knowledge, that each of us individually encounters when we care about those things. As a non-believer at 19 years old, I was absent-minded with no foresight on what might occur after death or whatever may occur in the applied scenario where I may transcend into higher realities. Having no liberation through knowledge and intellect, consequently, my being was damned to be consigned to the absent-minded realities that I frequented so often. These absent-minded realities coexisted in my mind. There existed no imagination or grandiose vision. Consequently, things got a little blurry in my subjective reality. I had no concept of an afterlife, other than that I was to go to Hell as a non-believer. It is clear these days, I had a working concept for the afterlife that was misguided. Therefore, I was thrown into an undeveloped void of mind for my spirit to take the opportunity to redirect and properly guide myself into higher consciousness.

"Hell is empty, and all the devils are here"
William Shakespeare

The next morning upon waking up, I had lost identity and subconsciously ushered in new perspective as a new being, a part of myself that I named Mark. No longer was I the same person that everybody was attached to. As rough as my identity crisis has been, it has also been rough for friends and family to understand Mark for who he is. Upon referring to Mark, please acknowledge I am speaking for not only myself, but for my alter-ego as well.

I became increasingly anxious as I observed the clock slowing down and speeding up, it felt broken, like time completely fell apart. My conscious being had been consumed with feelings of curiosity and fear. My coherence to reality and my perception were wobbling through space/time. The last two days were maddening, as it is unlikely to evade insanity in an environment known to induce it. It is a conundrum to work in a hospital that institutionalizes madness instead of exhausting it. I was very inquisitive with my applied intellect, putting an effort towards several observations in consideration of the relationship between physical reality and dimensions of time and how the two can fray away from each other. I was told I had the opportunity to speak to someone, anyone I thought. I asked to speak to Michael, one of my favorite strangers. The clinic failed to obtain his number, which is not a surprise.

They had a replacement TV up by the next day, and the room resumed use as a living space, as it would have with or without me. One of the other patients present with me told me to listen to my heart. That stuck with me, as I have never listened to my heart. I took his advice both literally and figuratively. Another day passed, and my stay at the mental hospital continued for a longer period than I anticipated. I needed to get out of there and get right in my head. On my final day, my state of mind deteriorated as I watched all the other patients leave and empty the place.

It was getting late into the night, and I could not tell what time it was. The fears I managed to suppress began to emerge, leaking from within my internalized imagination into the external world. A man who I assumed was a failed suicide attempt knew I was anxiously waiting to be released from the ward. It humored him to know I was having such a rough time. Though, this humor was not translated, and his intentions began to engulf his spirit. As my state of mind started to fall into the depths of Hell, I began to perceive Hell once again.

The man in front of me that was mocking me, his eyes started to glow and lime green trails started to pour from his eyes. As his body swayed following exhalations, dark smoke radiated from the outline of his body. I became frantic as they were beginning to turn on me. I had stayed for too long. I was being left behind; I had remained, convinced to believe. Feeling like I was stuck in this personal Hell, I began to cry heavily. A friend I adopted on an earlier day pulled me aside and talked me into playing a card game with him. I failed to keep my composure and fell apart, ready to give up. He pressured me into continuing to participate in this card game. Visitors I knew from my past life of sanity came for me. My mother and grandmother appeared on the other side of the glass. It did not take long for me to walk out of that nightmare. I went home after the three days of my stay.

I began to go mad through the gateway of my intelligence. I started obsessing over the fraction of one-third. I made an impulsive decision to repaint my room in cucumber green. I would not have chosen that shade of green had my mind been right. I conveyed my obsession of one-third in how I planned the interior painting. Roughly one-third of the room was white, and the rest was colored green. Later at night, I had a rough time fighting a lingering paranoia that I was being watched. I knew I was different because my mind bonded together my internal and external world. I felt incredibly vulnerable by the power of my mind, and pervasive fears crept their way into my every thought.

The TV at home was playing a television series, which was called Alcatraz, I believe. The setting started off within a prison and continued with a camera view passing along every cell. Foretelling the next scene through the story and visual cues, one would suspect a progression and change of scenes in the show. No, instead the show as I recall played the same scene repeatedly.

In continuing my attempts to gain something from this, I spent hours examining the interrelated relationship between perception and cognition. A relationship formed between my mind and living reality. I was insensible to schizophrenia and completely uninformed on mental illness. Before psychosis, I was entirely oblivious to altered states of consciousness – as all I that I had experienced in 2012 was foreign to me. The enigma of happenings consumed my entire being, and my intense fascination to understand more threw me into many more bouts of episodes.

"I must have broken the fourth wall," Mark thought to himself after reflecting and reviewing his recent experiences. The work of Father Time, directed by the incidental happenings of Mother Nature, had begun to acknowledge my existence. Words and sentences I heard from my outside sensory perception were synthesized into a different vocabulary only understood by my intuitive nature … which formed a foreign connection from my mind to collective reality.

Time is a mental construct as it sometimes functions as an imaginary time in equations. Transcending past the fourth dimension by breaking out of space/time in my mind, led me to the fifth dimension. The human mind is conditioned to work most effectively with computational sciences, as our mind performs the math and utilizes an array of proposed variables. The purpose of the relationship between the mind perceiving imaginary time and the fifth dimension is of pure speculation. I feel that this fifth dimension of space/time is in broad relationship to eternity.

My introduction to the fifth dimension put me in a loop of testing, evaluating, processing, and, ultimately, realizing. Upon my mind transcending the fourth dimension, time as a linear construct began to dissolve, becoming reduced to a pool of linear timelines intersecting within the geometries of the complex nature of space/time for the mind to perceive.

This meant more possibility in what could happen within a hallucinated, paradoxical nature of reality. Mark understood that his mind was simply "leaking" into his externalized reality. Imagined timelines of higher dimension were expressed in what only Mark could perceive. Feeling more vulnerable to possibility, Mark had to learn how to dominate his fears and alter his path while in this higher dimension of consciousness. He embarked on a new destiny, to chart a path into the higher dimensions for others to follow if they were to ever find themselves in this specific state of trance, it was the least Mark could do.

"Do not go where the path may lead, go instead
where there is no path and leave a trail."
Ralph Waldo Emerson

Foreign encounters with extraterrestrial beings occurred within the new interior domains of Mark's mind. Is it crazy to think that Mark took on the opportunity to form relationships with spiritual entities? Hallucinations come in all different forms, with every sense engaged. Sight, smell, touch, hearing, all blended into something reminiscent of a sixth sense.

Through strategizing his mind and developing a pseudointellectual system of mental technique, Mark attained the gift to exploit his hallucinations through manipulating his thoughts and could perceive his mind within reality. The heart is the guiding force in making conscious shifts of mind. With the effort of invested individual willpower, one can reduce possible timelines into one significant timeline of spiritual evolution. From birth to death, we live in one linear timeline, but we also all live in different timelines, and our timelines intersect within the fourth living dimension. Through settling his intentions of the heart, Mark began his journey to Heaven. Like most schizophrenics, Mark communed with spiritual entities and God. Mark did not gather much information from auditory voices. Instead, he found a source within.

In a lucid journey that occurred one night in a dream, Mark descended into deeper, more compacted dimensions. From flying across a planet to finding himself in a city amid a devastation. Mark got into an elevator and pressed the button to go down. As the elevator traveled down, gravity grew stronger. Mark's knees became weakened, forcing him to attempt walking while crouched.

Exiting the elevator, Mark found himself in a room full of very short people. The ceiling was positioned lower than usual. He sat on a sofa, taking in the experience momentarily. To the left he saw an opening, a door leading to something unimaginable. It was pouring radiant light into the room. Mark stood up and crouch-walked to the opening. At each side of the entrance to the light, he saw nutcrackers standing there guarding the white source of the unimaginable. Mark passed the wooden figures into an immersive environment of white energy with no real spatial definition. Upon waking up immediately, Mark understood this was Source – or at least the fringes of Heaven (perhaps the Gnostic Pleroma).

After a frightening and relatively traumatic experience in the first month of 2012, it is fair to say Mark exerted himself towards trying to align himself with the creator. Mark did not convert to Christianity, nor did he attempt to relate all he had experienced to one belief system. Religion is one central idea, divided into different perspectives that are understood through different historical narratives, often performed by sages, prophets, or other avatars.

Mark did not spend all his time alone; he infrequently spent quality time with his friends. That is, if you consider quality time as time where you spend muttering irrelevant thoughts to yourself, hoping your friends have input. At times, the friends did have something to offer. We all do. An experience can really shape a person, Mark knows this all too well. A good childhood friend of his avoided him during this period of his life. He was too alien to her, not the same individual she once knew. This is understandable, how can you have anything in common with a schizophrenic when you are not one? No, you do not relate, yet you share the same existence. And in the way of perception that the shaman sees the spirit world and its relationship with the real world, you ought to realize the same.

CHAPTER TWO

WITHIN THE RATIONAL MIND

Make use of your intuitive sensibility to empathetically identify the patterns of thoughts that I will construct within the framework of this book. We validate our curiosities through feeling, which stem from our fears and hopes. We determine what is false, by what we fail to conceive as true. However, much of the speculation within this book is intangible but holds a depth of purpose to be received by your mind.

Mark was involved in the church at a young age, as he was raised in a household embracing a lifestyle of Christianity. He identified with this upbringing from early pre-teenage years to mid-teenage years.

Mark served the role as an acolyte within the Church. Acolytes serve minor duties for the church congregation and perform a role in religious ceremonies. These duties involve walking the candlelight down to the altar and bringing light to the place of worship by passing the fire onto the candlesticks at the altar. Mark can recall walking down the aisle with aging eyes locked on his every footstep as he led the light into communion with the spirit of God. Mark also participated in Bible studies with his father, helping by offering his youthful perspectives on biblical texts. Seeking and ultimately finding Christ in Mark's spiritual journey failed early on, as he found no legitimacy within the claims made by the church. At 17 years old, Mark identified as atheist.

Does your mind only find truth through rationality? I will attempt to be persuasive of what is not widely accepted within the academic community, simply because there are not real answers out there yet. I will provide my conjecture to illustrate a different picture and purpose for you to reflect upon. This is all in my personal efforts to provoke deep thoughts and inspire curiosities deep within you. Helping you chart your direction is within my intentions.

What is not fully understood by our collective being spawns a curious nature within us to roam into territories unknown to our groupmind observation. When speculation is on the verge of recognition, we hypothesize and test for an outcome. As we are beings of self-inquiry, we are very interested in our intellectual potential. We react in opposition against the lifeless nature of the universe through our collective attempt to provoke deeper meaning and ascribe a sense of destiny. When we perceive light in a visual sense, we experience an innate curiosity to understand it. If the light is red, we think it must be warm. As creatures of observation, we touch the light to see the truth. Not much of hidden knowledge can be simply touched, so we tend to have blind faith in support of our beliefs. We will find a lot of our irrational suspicions about the nature of reality hold reasonable concern.

When provoking deep reflection within you, often you leave yourself pondering "what if?" as you encounter the indefinite capacity for possibilities within divine Nature. It is within your very nature to reflect upon the image of God within this seemingly endless universe. We excel towards mastery and a complete understanding. A question directed towards the divine mind will always give cause to some form of reaction. With the reaction comes the discovery of the divine infrastructure hidden away within reality. Helping permit your mind to experience and take control of altered states of consciousness takes conscious willpower.

Within your emotional being, you must develop an attitude and internal disposition. In reaction to this, your body's chemical composition changes into an alteration. This is received by the unconscious mind and your psyche adapts with your subconscious efforts to create a change within your energetic being. This alters your perception and consequently invokes change within the disposition of your conscious awareness, an altered state of consciousness.

In Marxian theory, the collective purpose of humankind is to create. In ideal social conditions, we evolve at incredible rates within the evolution of the mind. We are offered the opportunity to create a civilized kingdom, which is to be expressed from the depth of our imaginations. To put forth action into something ideological is very impressive, but to materialize this imagination is the work of God and divine creative Nature. We are to recreate and materialize the inner kingdom of Heaven into the physical world by expression of the divine.

You may experience cognitive dissonance throughout the reading of this book, simply because, you were taught through socialization to believe much about tangible reality. At any moment that I present a perspective that deeply conflicts with what you believe, you will be cognitively dissonant. Make efforts to reach beyond the limitations of your captivity held mind through subsumption of beliefs that undoubtedly control you. Making a shift in perspective takes an acrobatic mind. Please understand, that Heaven is entirely cognitively dissonant to what we presently understand through this world.

The scholar Max Weber offered theories that have influenced sociological perspectives and modern public administration. Weber also theorized about the thinking habits performed by deductive reasoning in our mind. Weber discussed four differing types of human rationality; I will inform you of two of the four types. The contrast between the two I present will show you the difference between the immediate perception of this world and a higher world found within the reasoning of speculation and possibility.

Practical rationality is the first of these two types of rationality I will present. The practical rationale is the critical thinking behind choosing to understand or reject something, for whether it is applicable or inapplicable to real-world interests. Is it practical? Does it have real-world applications? If the short answer is no, this method of reasoning will dispute the claims of much conjecture I put forth in this book. Those minds that are conditioned by practical rationality better not get ahead of themselves, because this form of rationality can obstruct the development of new thoughts, perspective, and ideas. Disputing the unknown is counterproductive. Practical rationality prevents insight from spawning within the framework of your basic intelligence. Many people are stubborn in this perspective and consequently will never understand through their own efforts what is not already explained by modern scientific findings.

It is entirely misguided willpower to shape and contour personal ideologies and self-interested beliefs to apply to standards of practical rationality. This form of rationality rejects extra dimensions and what is presently unknown until these concepts are structured and measured in a way that is pertinent to our observation. Much is not going to appear practical until you fully understand the functionality. Practical-rational thinkers progress in a way intellectually that leads them to distrust any great thinkers that intuitively adopt any form of theoretical conjecture.

If something appears too creative to exposit logic, practical-rational thinkers will react by rejection. This arguably is a handicap to the right creative hemisphere of the brain, which is often irrational anyways. Allowing yourself to obstruct the process of development in your thoughts by incessant use of practical rationality, is exactly what I want to avoid from you during the duration you spend reading this book.

We are taught the pragmatism of practical rationality during our youth, causing our imagination to submit to the tangible social realities we are told to believe in. From infancy to adulthood, we are told what is considered delusion and what is accepted by evidence. Limiting the creative potential in the developing minds of children prevents those minds from using their secondary intuitive intelligence. This handicaps the developing minds from comprehending patterns of creation and their imagination is arguably suppressed. Intuition serves as a compass for hidden wisdom that is found in the realm of the mind, it is critical thinking for comprehending the unconscious mind.

I ask of you to deconstruct your mind and suppress the intrusive attempts stemming from your socialized mind to see only practicality. It should also go without saying this is a spiritual book. Therefore, I cannot think your way for you towards any enlightened perspective. You must take the initiative to make acrobatic shifts of perspective in mind to discover much of this on your own. Move on from the limiting form of reasoning performed by practical rationality, as there is another development of reasoning known as theoretical rationality.

Theoretical rationality sustains objectivity, as it serves the purpose to master reality through increasingly abstract and complex thoughts. Structuring thoughts, in theory, is bidirectional in process. You may work backwards from the ideation of Heaven to the beginning of Nature, or you may structure your thoughts from the progression of Nature into the product of Heaven. Sorcerers, sages, prophets, theoretical scientists, and great thinkers all utilize theoretical rationality.

Please understand, the way into appreciating this book is by embracing this equipped form of rationality. If you are the type of person to skip to the evidence with supporting reference material, you are not going to like my presentation and will end up frustrated simply because this book is not easy to understand. The advances and discoveries of scientific theory are simply not enough for the proper speculation necessary to explain the material in this book. This book explores the hidden worlds and the metaphysics that guide the actions of the universe and Nature.

Rationality equipped mankind with the right knowledge for directing the investments of effort through deciding what is beneficial or not for individual gain. If you have ever attempted to communicate something you have understood, yet another person has not, usually that person fails to see your perspective. Typically, they are applying a conflicting form of rationality that devalues the substance of your argument. Unfortunately, most people are practical-rational thinkers, and, sadly, that is all that they can do. A pragmatic approach to lifestyle leads to the philosophical orientation of existential nihilism.

A mind that is trained to work practically will never exhaust its effort to see into the irrational Nature of reality. Departures from rationality can take you into the theoretical reach of proximity to God. The omnipotent and immaterial consciousness that is God is residing in the irrational realities of Heaven. For an intellectual nomad, something that appears unrealistic is only an opportunity to be understood by deeper insights. We can become closer to God when we resolve our biggest questions. All that separates us from God is that the omniscient being knows and we do not know yet.

Agnosticism is a process of self-evaluation. Tendencies of agnosticism emerge from within when the pragmatic mind begins to retract influence over consciousness. As the pragmatism becomes less intrusive to our thinking habits, the rational mind regresses back into its original creative nature – an open mind. Imagination as an essence finds formation from the untapped potential of the unconscious mind. As most of an iceberg is submerged in the arctic water, much of our spiritual intelligence is untapped and incoherent to the active mind.

If you choose to continue counterproductive thinking and dispute my ideas and concepts within your mind without putting effort into reflection, you will be passed by other minds that remain passive by understanding. You will be left by those who transcend your lower-conscious attitude of mind. They will leave you because you do them no good. You keep them as they are and expect nothing more, hoping that they agree with your every word which progresses to no outcome. It is fine to work with presented evidence, but if you never thought about what it all may amount to, then you have failed to remain objective. The evolution of science existed before us and our present understanding, therefore, don't forecast it leads to nowhere, do not stop before your imagination. Accepting that modern scientific evidence and reasoning is incomplete, there is nothing illogical about choosing not to be pragmatic about something when you are completely aware that so many ideas remained undiscovered.

Within the rational mind is the progressive development of the soul, facing the trivial circumstances of investigating the unknowns of hidden Nature. With knowledge comes opportunity, how you engage yourself with the knowledge outlines the karmic orientation of your being. As an author, I will tell you half-truths by rhetoric, as I believe you are fully capable of conceiving a completed picture through the echoes of your mind. There is more to the question of an afterlife because there are many angles to be factored. After so much perspective, you begin to perceive the riddle of our cosmic drama. I shun the deception that I know all the answers, as I accept the truth that I grapple with every day, which is that I suck at riddles.

However, I can identify that most of the existential and inherent purpose is discovered within the riddle we understand to be the enigma of life. For stubborn minds, people insist upon learning the hard way and take many steps in the wrong direction. All signs may point west, but after following one direction or mode of life, you will be east of where you once stood. It is pertinent to your developing intuitive evolution that you keep to a progressive spirituality. As a collective, we need much more reflection and reevaluating. We are traumatized by being left with no truth, purpose, or reasoning for our existence. The best may be brought out of us, yet in poor self-esteem, we tend to develop destructive behaviors and ideologies.

Many denominations of religion stand apart from the collective in their independent subculture, characterized by more specific theological opinions. These religious institutions do this, by becoming too "wrapped up" into a common mind that is foreign to the collective group mind. Isolating the numerous group identities within the collective forms a barrier of empathy between one group with another. This brings much consequence as the failure of empathy results in the destruction of humanity.

To transcend mind into a transcendental reality, you no longer resist evolutions of the soul – meaning, you no longer reject the evolutions of your psyche and psychic development. There is popular belief that it takes dissolution of egoic identity to transcend this reality. That is a half-truth but also functions as a compete misconception to those who take everything quite literally. Your objective should not be restraining your personality and in result flattening your mood. Those deceived think they must be entirely dehumanized to acquire real insights. My advice as an alternative is to no longer allow yourself to strictly adhere to the rigid nature of social norms. If the world shapes you, you are inferior in mind by the pervasive fears of this world. If you instead are shaped by spirit, you are superior to the relentless suffering of this world.

Empathy as another form of feeling is an art form of spiritual practice. With empathy, you can accomplish many magical things. You may know how a person is feeling in the moment, understanding what is on their mind and in their heart. You can use your emotional intelligence to help heal their emotional trauma.

Mark has had a few encounters with other people, where he has utilized his empathy in practice. The gift is to empathetically identify the thoughts and feelings of another individual. Allow yourself to be reminded that the feelings of another are like the feelings of yourself. Within yourself, project your emotional being into the arena of the emotion of another individual. Feel their feelings, take steps in reaction to those feelings. Guide their being with the words and perspective that is necessary to take their hurting heart into a higher perspective of meaning and light.

Let me enlighten you on myself as an author, as it will explain a bit when it comes to my writing style. My mind jumps from point to point, and it does not connect the dots as much as it identifies those dots. I express the bigger picture regarding my writing, hoping that you find it veridical in an alternative headspace. I hope that perhaps my vague descriptive science of reality touches upon one of the alternative ways you sometimes choose to perceive reality. Enlightened states of mind help you achieve a perception in which reality feels much like a digital simulation, a coordination of events that draw people into a grand scheme, which is to say a heavenly discourse.

This chapter serves the purpose to better prepare your critical thinking and inform your mind, so that you may process the content of this book. A heavenly discourse stems from the unthinkable through the divine intentions of the pervasive imagination of Nature.

I will tell you seemingly irrational lessons, for example, Nature has an imagination. From realizing its depth of imagination, creation actualizes from its source of conception. A heavenly discourse is the process of enlightenment. Realize, reflect, process, actualize, invent, redirect, and complete in perfection, in a process of evaluation to guide yourself through the conscious evolving realities of Nature and the hidden worlds.

CHAPTER THREE

PRACTICING AWARENESS

Practicing awareness is developing a new form of awareness through recreating your perception of reality in your mind, allowing you to attract new heights of consciousness. How you perceive your social interactions with this reality, and how you perceive this world system can be brought to higher domains of conscious reality. Synthesizing the lessons and events in your life into messages which Nature may be attempting to communicate allows you to advance into a whole new context of life to derive meaning from.

Evading the suffering of this world is best served through the practice and philosophy of escapism, by engaging into alternate perceptions of reality as a means of enjoying fantasies. Heaven, or fantasies, are simply differing interpretations for why things are the way they are. Forming a heightened reality in the conscious mind requires a complex system of perception utilizing levels of the mental, physical, and spiritual. Participating in social interactions offers a medium of communication, allowing you to gain awareness of the present ever-evolving conception of the meaning of life. Through your conversations with others, continually make effort to seek deeper meaning and higher awareness. The revealing of your calling will happen throughout the process of your heart finding love for a role in God's plan.

From the depths of the abyss, we were raised by spirit to incarnate physical vessels to immerse ourselves within an imagination of our own making. You are caught in a non-physical and intelligent matrix only to seek answers of higher purpose.

The process of evolution has archetypal significance. Evolution is a linear course of development, characterized by an increasing complexity of Nature to serve some meaningful purpose in the sphere of life within the universe. In the metaphor of evolution, we were brought from nothing into something at the mere calling of the divine. The quintessential meaning found within the processes of life have lessons invested within them for us to interpret and learn.

In this matrix of physical reality, the perceived reasoning for our lives and the events within our life perpetually shift in perspective depending on where you place yourself by reaction. Embracing a victim mentality causes you to feel and empathize with your pain.

Your mentality is the characteristic attitude of your mind. The concept of a 'state of mind' is similar, but instead of simply being an attitude, it is the psychospiritual disposition of mind. Embracing a psychospiritual disposition within your expressed being develops a gateway between the spirit and the expression of you. As it is your human vehicle that is perceiving an expression of reality as result of your brain chemistry, the gateway continues past limitations as an influential force of your observed reality.

Higher consciousness and transcendental reality are a product of your internalized psychospiritual predispositions. A realistic, pragmatic approach to reality creates a boundary between practical perceptions of reality and a higher-ordained reality of pure theoretical speculation. Anything beyond the face of this matrix is a complete theory, simply conjecture provided by unsubstantiated logic. The right hemisphere of the brain takes kindly to the imagination. Half of our mind is developed imagination, a parallel dimension of mind that is an alternative expression of our living experience. The worlds that exist within our mind are immaterial, but they hold their own dimension. Inventors express into reality through replicating the dimensions of the imagination in their thoughts brought together.

God expressed the creation of us by the development of the universe. In a literary context of imagination, out of nothing came the story of our created universe. And it evolves in a way that connects all meaning within creation. This literary development may be perceived by us as an evolving story or drama, a cosmic drama. From the absence of existence, comes the archetypal reality that is constructed on vague abstract representations and concepts. This form of reality is known as Atziluth, term coined by Jewish mystics. An example would be the archetypal characters known to us through astrology and the literary context of the stars above. There is the hero, the serpent, the bearer of wisdom, and so on.

Each archetype provides a general outline creating a vague sense of character. There are manifestations of each archetype. Each manifestation holds finer details from being the evolution of a mere concept. I will make future reference to Atziluth because it is a fundamental part in the process of creation. The collective imagination is evolved and created through the Four Worlds known in Jewish mysticism.

From our imagination into the first world, Atziluth, we create characters from the void into complete pictures and personalities. The cosmic drama functions to create a literary, descriptive reality, providing a context from which things behave, act, and grow upon. Of the second world, Briah, the character within ourselves gains self-awareness and begins to sense for a direction in space/time, a direction into the future of unfolding events. Though, at this development, there is not yet shape nor form.

The cosmic drama is aware, and it breathes imagination. In Yetzirah, the third world of Formation, the created of the imagined takes shape and form. At this level of creation, we are cognitively dissonant from our inherent origins of non-existence. We develop a sense for ego in the subjective experience. At last, we are completed within creation at the level of Assiah, the fourth world of Action. We are entitled to character, a sense of direction, and an ego. With action, we become karmic beings which operate "as above, so below" in a spiritual realm of creation. At the seemingly non-spiritual and physical level, we are entities of the physical Assiah, the Assiah Gashmi.

The evolving, manifesting, linear timeline we concern as our present reality is creative non-fiction much like this book, ironically. Within everyday scenarios, there exists a literary context that forms and develops in the direction of future space/time events. Meaning is created by everyday situations and is the driving force that furthers the development in the story of creation. As Yetzirah is existence versus the non-existence of Briah, we reflect upon non-existence. We are as characters in this young mythological era of creation.

Ervin Goffman, a micro-level sociologist, looked within our social interactions to inquire what motivates action within the collective people. He theorized how we create micro-level social realities. We participate within reality in social situations as an

actor in what Goffman has termed as The Interaction
Order.

The evolving heavenly discourse that has a source
in the creation of the universe is a cosmic literary
drama that involves us as actors. Like Greek theatre
and drama, there exists a literary narrative and context
within our everyday life that may be examined. We
create a context, a social composition that incorporates
our feelings, thoughts, and actions.

*"We are all just actors trying to control and
manage our public image, we act based on how
others might see us."*
Ervin Goffman

We interact through symbolic interactionism.
Mirror neurons communicate with each other in our
minds to synthesize a relationship between
psychology and the physical framework of the living
universe. The creation of bees and their level of
communication when forming together a beehive is
symbolic of the way we function as observers. We
understand that natural sciences can complement each
other in a sort of paradigm of nature.

Our communication extends past the words we
speak by the projections of our mind within the living
intelligent universe. We release signals in a variety of
forms to inform the universe and each other about our
status regarding harmony. These signals could be
called bad vibes something felt by spiritualists and

surfer bros. Intention is a passive force that is communicated by the metaphysical nature in the dimension of mind.

Human elitists have driven humankind throughout many ages of development. At times their intentions were for complete control, but at other times, elitists have worked together for progress. Elitists tend to be consumed in an obsession to master whatever brings the most fulfillment.

Modern elitists have learned to warp our perceptions of reality through the manipulation of what are called 'social structures'. To practice awareness, you would need to be willing to read through this portion of the chapter to gain understanding that the way to spiritual progress, will be different than the way of the world, a global system. We will reflect on important sociological concepts, which will inform our perspective of how this matrix of social conditions can decline in quality of morality.

Our collective society has adopted religious social structures to preserve social control. These dominant social structures hold power over our life and suppress free will. The major world religions tend to condition the individual behavior of religious communities by the theory of Interaction Order. These believers of whichever God act appropriately to the 'divine standard' held in place by devotion to dogmatic belief systems. These socially constructed collective belief systems ultimately shape the way we interact and behave. The human behavioral psychology that has been conditioned by a predictable belief system becomes predictable human social interaction. A limited worldview perpetuates the submissive belief we have no control. We lack autonomy in how to evolve from the predictable into the unpredictable.

Unevolved social structures that are rigid and distort our perceptions of one another tend to limit our spiritual and psychic evolution. Unevolved religion becomes outdated. This unevolved state of religion becomes repressive towards the evolution of human spirituality. It structurally negates the condition in which human consciousness expands towards another evolution of awareness.

Religion did not exist as a word in earlier eras of humankind. Organized religion is an ideological tool to impose harsh judgments onto other people as result of moral questioning and moral dilemma. Religion was used in those ways during the colonial history of Western civilizations. A religious mindset is repressed by dogma, consequently operating on lower planes of mind where communication suffers.

Elitist infiltrators of our society are equipped with the knowledge of how installing impenetrable social structures can mediate groupmind behavior and develop predictable behavior in the population, for example, organizing a religious belief system to form networking among the common minds of everyday people. Then, they can, control that subpopulation by anointing a religious leader to command them. The relationships of networking between religious leaders and secret elitist societies direct the mass populations of people through the social transformations of demographic transitions using Hegelian dialectical theory to create increasing order among the instability of a poorly treated society.

In efforts to prevent the proletariat working class from organizing an intellectual revolution, the elitists have a variety of strategies. Corporations keep the vital energy of society drained, by distracting the population through an onslaught of consumerism. Sensationalist actors and comedians deny the impression that the situation is serious and instead offer bad humor and comedy relief to desensitize the world to tyrannies.

Through social theory, embodied tyranny can direct the public into serving a discourse of unfolding calamities. These times of distress deteriorate the emotional well-being and incite chaotic behavior. Through creating the ideal conditions, mankind's original state of nature can be perverted and begin to stray from higher consciousness. Aristocratic culture is grounded in the role to command efforts of the working class in the social system. Enslaving the human mind begins with 1) dominating the mind with thoughts and desire and 2) controlling free-will so humans act and behave predictably.

A warden is an administrative position for an individual with the necessary intelligence to direct social operations. There are social wardens infiltrating modern America.

Mental planes are stratified based on degrees of consciousness. The mental planes lacking in conscious awareness tend to serve the more animalistic primal nature of self. This develops a struggle between the intentions of the isolated minds of lower consciousness and those with the liberty of unconstrained thinking. We all fend for our happiness within a conflict between learned (or possibly internalized) worldly desires, and our inner intuitive and creative aspirations.

The inner childlike self aspires to be, and in reaction, the aging soul receives inspiration to find how to be. From this, we are inspired by creation. Though, we are often handicapped by only finding a reason to dwell in the familiar world. The inner childlike self must always aspire beyond this world into the unimaginable. This is fundamental in ascension. Going beyond the familiar is outside the comfort zone for many because it entails changing the very nature of yourself. Either repress yourself to be dependent upon reasoning or go beyond reasoning into what is inspired by feeling.

Not everything will make sense. While continuing the journey into Heaven, you will begin to tap into what truly makes sense. The disconnection between yourself and your heart will be resolved. It is pure ecstasy to live in an alternative headspace where all feeling is put into expression, where emotions are not shallow, and everything is done with positive intention. We are at a loss for what was intended for our existence, but we create meaning when we intend for the best. We are victims of a social system developed by social wardens. Therefore, we must build a temple within for spiritual nourishment. In ideal conditions of spirit, the evolution of spirit comes naturally. Altering your perception of the world system into a separate reality of your own making allows you to create the conditions that promote individual growth.

There are many levels of consciousness. The biotic intelligence known as cellular life communicate through chemical signals. Through this, relationships are formed from the functions of the body. The brain operates as a groupmind to perform the administrative role to facilitate the workings of cellular life. The networking of cell life has a relationship to the functions of our mind.

In our brain are mirror neurons that develop synchronicity between the different minds of people. The experiments of brain imaging show that the human inferior frontal cortex and superior parietal lobe are active when the person acts and when the person sees another individual acting. A sort of entanglement through empathy occurs between two like minds and may extend to a circle of like-minded people. The web of social interaction and empathetic entanglement develops the web of human collective groupmind consciousness.

As a social collectivity, groupmind operates collective intelligence through the configuration of networking, connecting all the different minds of individuals. We can access this dimension of groupmind, by discovering it through altered states of consciousness.

The photographs of the recorded universe seem to mimic the imagery found within the neural network of the brain. This universe has a resemblance to the brain and may be termed as the universal mind or divine mind. This divine mind is the ascended form of each part of the human collective groupmind, also involving other intelligent species and beings in the universe. Occurring within every brain ever conceived in the universe are the noetic entanglements of the common mind in the relationship of mental dimension with the universal divine mind.

The relationships between the many levels of consciousness are the gateway by which we communicate with the higher divine. The divine mind is the intelligent framework of the living universe. It is the intelligent source of conception. Through mathematics, a product of human rationality, we develop a relationship with the living universe. Our engaged minds understand the mathematical language that shapes the functions of the physical universe. The divine mind is both the indirect and direct source of intelligence that reproduces the scientific nature of reality, through a cyclical manifesting singularity of awareness. If anything has the potential to make logical sense, there is always a possibility that it is manifested or will be manifested. The struggle for any practical-rational mind is that the individual would have to understand that this intelligence is untraceable and invisible but does exert influence over any form of evolving intelligence. Reality is the culmination of forces found within the source of natural sciences and creative Nature. That is, things grow to become smarter, mutate, and become multifaceted.

Evolution is a process that affects everything. There exist evolutions of human consciousness which can be perceived when looking at the historical transformations of art. Art is a medium for expressing the higher divine realities understood by our subconsciousness. Prehistoric civilization was proud to find and create fire, but that required development to occur within the awareness of consciousness to happen. It has been said before that gross evolution of the human body has been completed; we will no longer grow a third arm. Now, we are to intellectually evolve into higher consciousness, which will ultimately manifest from natural intelligence to spiritual intelligence. Before every evolution is a pressure point that is triggered (or stressed) to create results.

Human existentialism must pass these pressure points to evolve in conscious awareness. We are facing a mirror that is symbolic of the universe. We see the potential of the universe manifested and realized. We realize in enlightenment that we are to be like the universe. We have an eternity to evolve and to transcend, to grow as beings of light into higher domains of the mind. Like the universe, we are also magnificent in potential and conceived with greatness in the image of God. We have the wisdom within us; it is simply untapped by the available information of the incoherent mind.

Existential crises are rooted in the slow death of your identity. You have latched onto the temporary and the human identity, like everyone else you know. You are transitioning into the eternal, into the undefinable, journeying through the night of the soul. You will find that you are eternal and completely present within yourself. The existential crisis you experience is simply trained fear from being taught that time ceases to exist.

There is no time; there are only present moments within the fourth-dimensional hallways of the universe. Only present moments that take place in the past or future exist, which are both simply directions in the fourth living dimension. The future and past indicate a progression or regression of events. As we conduct conscious action and make changes to the reality we are engaged in, we may change our relationship to the dualistic nature of our reality. This ultimately changes the discourse of evolution with the self, which changes us. As karmic beings of the physical Assiah, we naturally live in the consequence of the karma we create. What is in the question of 'right' or 'wrong'? It is in the question of what idolization or deity you are defining your service to.

Each mind engages the collective social reality through a few former elementary functions of perception.

1. Identification, the process of becoming personal and familiar.
2. Association, the relationship perceived with all else.
3. Symbolism, the interpreted creative features invested in material reality.
4. Past engagements, the lessons learned through previous hallways of time.

Within the parameters of each function, the content of our engaged reality is managed through:

1. Classification
2. Characterization

In classification, experiences and relationships are categorized within the subconscious. In characterization, the egoic force is interpreted and defined by your affiliations.

This perception adds the necessary literary elements to form a narrative. Furthermore, as perception is symbolic, it may be used to reason information out of one moment or situation such as wisdom and understanding. With an active imagination, you can perceive the inner contents of a spoken sentence, and parse the tone of voice for information, creating points of reference to correspond with emotion. This practice is paralinguistic. You can understand the meaning and inner context of what is communicated through the timing of spoken words and the pitch of words being spoken. The expressed words of another individual are always a reflection of their emotional state and awareness. This can develop into a complex practice of knowing another individual's feelings and thoughts in more detail.

The archetypal mind operates in many ways to display a sense of character stemming from the ego. This allows us to present ourselves in a way that is characteristic of our inner self. For some people, they have yet to discover what is within them. For others, after finding a higher identity exists within, they become that character and quit acting. However, very few go on to be directors and creators. Celestial archetypal identities are found within the inspiring hearts of many and some of those people have awakened to the realization and take it seriously.

There exist many trends in creation other than the celestial variety, as any strain foreign to the human nature is best understood as being extraterrestrial consciousness. As actors playing roles within our social realities, we are perceived by groupmind as figures of history and the future. This may be why we continue to regard good and evil through memory. It is an effort of collective groupmind to recognize patterns of behavior psychology as performed by the morality of individuals. Lurking within the imagination of collective groupmind are all our conceptions of spirit phenomenon.

Different minds communicate together by associating between symbols, images, and other types of information. After death, we leave an imprint on Earth's history, which that image devolves into myth. We are all neutral by intelligent design, possessing both characteristics of good and evil. In liberty, we are blessed with the opportunities to express and define our willpower. You will either travel the galaxies adopting new forms of evil or give life and a wealth of knowledge to others. This is the inevitable outcome of creation, and I have faith mankind will survive the devils and increasingly bleak future.

Intelligence is a viral phenomenon that rapidly evolves effected vessels and spreads from one to another. Our intelligence is extraterrestrial in origin, forming from a galactic consciousness. We stream intelligence through the archetypal mind as it entangles the mental reality of metaphysical emanation with the physical world. Liberation of flesh is the beginning of all we can look forward to. Though, avoid understanding death as the grim reaper, as he will only depress you. Death asking you to surrender your possessions, leave your loved ones, and move past your life … for what?

We are present within the mind of God, participating through roles of his created imagination. The decision to personify God is your own choice, as it does not make much difference if you fail to perceive him correctly. In the mind and heart of God he sees his manifestations destined for greatness. The divine Almighty acts through the quintessential definition held within the context and meaning of reality. If you could imagine a sequence of unfolding events and imagine a change in direction, the principal cause for that change of direction is the main point of intervention by the divine Almighty. Forming a mutually beneficial relationship with God is important to spiritual evolution, as he acts as a catalyst for progression.

"In the beginning, God created the heavens and

the Earth."

(Genesis 1:1)

This heavens within your mind, what comes of it? Many people will say it is after death in an afterlife. No, no, I dispute that. We are on Earth and the heavens reign above our gazes, the clouds, the moon, and the stars, in the vast space environment where all neighboring galaxies call home. We were created, evolved to master ourselves and practice our willpower within the living universe. The scripture of Genesis calls the universe the 'heavens', which does include the higher echelons of heaven in the higher, more complex dimensions of space and time. This should happily be embraced with gratitude, as the universe and its scientific evolution are quite marveling.

Much of atheism rejects creation in these ways because of 'magic', seeing it as something very superstitious, delusional, and impossible. It may be interpreted that creation is all around us and is simply expressed through levels of natural sciences to create life eventually. In this perspective, it comes easily to personify the universe as a creator. I contend that no religious group is right or wrong, all wisdom can shape the soul in different ways. In practicing awareness, you seize opportunities to grow instead of choosing to be ignorant. In the history of the greatest scholars who have walked the Earth, their minds and thoughts would not have transpired to conclude there may be something when there is nothing.

Atheism as discussed is the outcome of practical rationality. There are no real-world applications for belief systems that worship gods. Therefore, it is not practical or reasonable to believe. However, in theoretical rationality, the theory may progress to allude to an outcome of godly circumstances. You may find it takes more effort to rationalize the irrational rather than to simply debate the irrational.

How may I evolve within a belief system of my own making? If you were to read religious texts for guidance, choose to look deeper into the exegeses of scripture with an esoteric lens for traces of divine conspiracy. Jesus spoke in metaphors and parables to guide the sheep into paradise. In John 14:2, Jesus Christ says,

"My Father's house has many rooms; if that were not so, would I have told you that I am going there to prepare a place for you?"

Jesus Christ

Shed off whatever conceptions you may have been taught, as your pastor may have been illegitimating in his interpretation. Let go of the opinions you feed from others that have dehumanized wise teachers as perpetuators of dogma. Jesus spoke of Sephirot within the Tree of Life, referring to them as "rooms" in the sense of metaphor. He was blessed with the intellect to traverse these metaphysical realms of thought as described by Jewish mysticism. With no basis of theoretical physics, Jewish mystics managed to identify the existence of metaphysical realms. Mind you, these realms of a mental dimension may also correspond with the projections of the theoretical physical dimensions in the real world.

The lower levels of the Sephirot exist within the material dimension of reality. The kingdom is within you, the heavens above, and here we are on Earth. The quagmire of our existence fades away in memory as we are equipped to become knowledgeable, spiritual, and intellectual geniuses that take on the campaign of enlightenment throughout the universe. The kingdom of Heaven is embedded within your neural network. As mentioned, Sephirot are the circles illustrated in the Kabbalist Tree of Life.

Each Sephirah is ascribed characteristics, meanings, energetic qualities, and metaphysical properties. Eternally they reside within you and your mind. Mentor yourself through a higher conscience of Self. With mental effort, kinesthetically learn the ability to traverse to these higher planes of thought within the divine mind. Ein Sof manifests these realms of mind and forms metaphysical dimension holding knowledge. In all sephirot, is a source of divine light energy known as 'Ohr'. The light energy gives the creative process to the inner-dimensional Nature of each sephirah. As light enters the mind, energy vibrates to develop images. From images comes an inspired imagination.

State of Mind, the main objective I have taken on to impart to you, is the access key to these higher realms of reality. A state of mind is a subtle, spiritual state and internal disposition of heart, which inspires activity, motivations, and intentions to be tapped by the conscious awareness. A state of mind is a psychospiritual disposition of mind.

Command the active effort to discover these underlying subconscious states of social realities existing within groupmind by provoking source energy from within through an altered state of mind. This activates the hidden regions of mind and offers access to unlock information of the repressed unconscious mind, the information that streams through the expressed creative mind and imagination. You can mine the intelligent framework of your mind for new life lessons, hidden knowledge of the occult, and acquire skills and abilities.

A state of mind is performed by a motivation you feel, which corresponds to a psychological state in the perceived human spiritual experience. Navigating through different states of mind, you can locate these cognitive realms of thought. In corresponding the energies, activities, and qualities from a sephirah to yourself, you can link your mind to its Ohr, the source energy that enlightens the mind. Ohr appears from the Ayn Sof Ohr, which is what I call Source in my New Age-like methodology. This source is an all-natural singularity of infinite information, best described as bright, white light. A light so bright, and full of every color, that it transcends color information into a spectacular white energy. Source emanates from within the divine mind and is shaped by the impressions left by passive individual minds.

For each different sephirah is an associated state of mind, which an individual can engage in to perceive the specific inner contents of reality within the concealed nature of absolute reality. From engagement of Chokmah, wisdom appears to the observer out of nothingness. Wisdom is esoteric, as it is knowledge by revelation. Within the content of a symbolism or situation is contained a stream of information from which we receive inner meaning. Wisdom and the understanding that comes from within the mind typically is reflected by your heartfelt dispositions, or, your morality. This can change the outcome of how the information is received.

The third eye or pineal gland functions as a photoreceptor. The pineal gland intercepts light waveforms and stores data. The processing of the data informs the pineal gland how much melatonin to administer to give us a proper day-night sleep cycle. Falling asleep is easier at night because the pineal gland relays information that there are low light levels which put the mind to rest. Melatonin also induces creative states, provoking deep imaginations which incur dreaming states that are weird and abstract. Melatonin regulation may have to do with us having a grip on reality.

The pineal gland perceiving light leaves impressions on the brain. The pineal gland is a mechanism of consciousness. In our unconscious states we know the physical senses are suppressed and the mind wanders. Instead of concluding our consciousness is *shut off* – let us consider that instead, the mind is *turned on* and that we begin to experience the mental dimension of reality rather than the physical dimension.

The pineal gland perceives infrared light. At low vibrations, this can induce a variety of emotions including sleeplessness, crying, agitation, and depression. At higher vibrations, it induces positive moods. Hidden with the pineal gland as an organ is "the seat of the soul" as you may have heard in Cartesian philosophy. I have corresponded 'soul' in this book with what I believe is its equivalent, which is the *psyche*. The pineal gland is the lens of the hidden mental reality. As we have understood, the pineal gland has a level of control over our emotional temperaments through the processing of light information. If anything, this tells us that our soul, or psyche, has a relationship with the way we perceive reality. Consequently, that relationship which influences our moods is differentiated by the higher and lower vibrations of light.

The third eye chakra has an association with the sephirot of Chokmah and Binah. At the level of psyche and soul, the third eye is in a relationship with Da'at, the hidden sephirah. Da'at is the sephirah for 'knowledge' or 'consciousness' and we know Chokmah and Binah are the Sephirot for wisdom and understanding. Da'at is the conscious power of intellect, forming from wisdom and understanding. Chokmah and Binah synthesize together wisdom and understanding into the knowledge of Da'at. Therefore, our third eye receives understanding and wisdom which creates a sense of knowledge that is expressed in the hidden sephirah of Da'at. This means receiving wisdom and understanding generates knowledge and consciousness, which is an awakening. Da'at also holds the function of memory and recognition, which furthers its association with the third eye, the gateway to the soul, the psyche that is developed by conscious awareness.

In the occult belief-system of Thelema, the progression of achieving the hidden or unawakened sephirah of Da'at is through passing an ego-death. When the sense of self and identity is deconstructed, the soul begins to appear in our vessel instead. We become who we truly are inside, instead of being a byproduct of a socially constructed matrix. Da'at is accessed through the synthesis of wisdom and understanding, which helps an individual gain recognition of hidden realities and the ability to perceive them due to sensitivity. Accessing the Da'at through the probing of the third eye allows the ability to mine intelligence from the inner dimensions of higher reality. In Kabbalah, Da'at operates on two different levels of knowledge. At one level, there is the Da'at Elyon which is higher knowledge. The lower level of Da'at involves the emotional intelligence of the soul and is known as Da'at Tachton, meaning lower knowledge.

As the pineal gland has a connection with our emotional state and wellbeing, it is also involved with Da'at Tachton for our emotional intelligence. Awakening of higher reality from passing through a death of ego, allows the psyche to perceive reality in a new vision. With increasing emotional intelligence from the synthesized knowledge of wisdom and understanding, the psyche can unlock the upper level of Da'at Elyon which is connected to Keter, the sephirah of higher divine light. From this upper level, we gain through reflection the information of higher knowledge, also known as hidden knowledge. Keter is associated with the crown chakra, which correlates us to the receptive nature of the divine mind, the universe.

The cloak of mystery that surrounds the unknown is a hint to the inner Sephirah of Da'at (knowledge). When you perceive mystery, it is simply shrouded knowledge. What you do not presently know is without mystery because you lack awareness of it. Become aware of what still perplexes you with mystery and tackle that mystery with the willpower to understand.

The pineal gland behaves as a gateway for the perception of reality and our relationship to it. It is the centerfold of both creative and logical mind merging egoic identity with the psyche. The psyche creates a metaphysical sense of self and identity as an entity of a social environment. A mind that is engaged notices patterns by association that influence the outcomes of Nature. We can see patterns that also relate self with Nature because we are an identity within Nature. Evolution is a natural process that comes in many expressions. It is the process of increasing intelligence.

We all say that everyone has the same God, but we willingly kill each other over religion and our differences. All organized religion alludes to the same God through constructions of worldview with the foundation of culture. Each religion exists within a dimension of mind. Metaphysics are the theoretical constructs that integrate physical reality with the mental reality. Things like identity, time, being, substance and space develop a dimension within our minds through our perceptions of the world.

Geographic location is the reason why so many people have different identifying religions of the same Abrahamic or whichever religion. They see either what they were taught or what they have reasoned for the most part. God is a multidimensional being that emanates throughout existence and the fabric of space/time.

The dissonance between the rulings of Heaven and the worldly affair of Earth is because mankind has failed to understand the consequences of knowing both good and evil. The failure to adhere to natural forces within Nature and seeking harmony keep the conscience of collective groupmind in perpetual suffering. A select number of Jews identify Satan as the force of ego, the force of egoic tendency is a teacher that allows us to draw a contrast between the duality of knowledge.

We are to obtain the knowledge that understanding may serve us, but also the wisdom that we are to serve others. Ego is the vehicle of identity that helps us learn. It teaches us the reflective nature of willpower and the universe, and those natural consequences come as a reaction. We are simply being taught the elementary functions of higher ordained existence from the forces of Nature. The channelings of the

Egyptian God Ra from the book *Law of One*, seem to allude to the invested capabilities of each soul.

> *"The technology of which you, as a social complex, are so enamored at this time is but the birthing of the manipulation of the intelligent energy of the sub-Logos which, when carried much further, may evolve into technology capable of using the gravitic effects of which we spoke."*
>
> *The Law of One*

I am not going to interpret this literally as if it is with technology that we will make remarkable progress, though that may also be an outcome. I believe what is being communicated here is we are all beings of incredible intelligent design. Therefore, by manipulating the intelligent energy of our lesser self, we may evolve into beings of exceptional design with the capability to achieve things of "gravitic" effects.

What kind of effects might those be? Manipulation of the physical environment and the higher dimensions, perhaps, even by the mental projections of our psychic interactions with Nature. Ra is talking as if the capacity to do such is invested within us. Though, this is all my interpretation. Either way, we must remember that the way towards an ascension would be to motivate ourselves from the core of our being.

The caterpillar excites his muscles from within the cocoon, working to break out of his shell. This shell can also serve as a casket if the caterpillar fails to defeat the illusions of his entrapment. By believing in more, and pushing forward, the caterpillar motivates his whole being to fight and ultimately break free from the cocoon to become a butterfly, a monarch. The archetypal world source of reality Atziluth is creating a descriptive sense of the truth about the evolutionary nature of reality. Atziluth is teaching us that though we may be covered in a blanket of darkness at the end of our lives as human beings, we will make a conscious break out of shape and form into spatially undefined beings of spirit. Humanity is the final step of Earth in the spiritual transmigration from lesser lifeforms into higher conscious lifeforms. At the end of a satisfactory life, we will exit into another chapter of eternity.

Ego works to teach us that serving one perspective suppresses the development of many perspectives within Nature. The ego is there to confuse you into directing your efforts from within to the outside as if expressing your frustrations make fundamental change. Expression of those energies within the psyche, allows the intrinsic force of Nature to express fundamental change. From within occurs the process of mind, and without mind is spirit. Therefore, the spirit is the natural expression of self.

A moral conscience that is repressed by egoic and nonempathetic perspectives, and a superior sense of self, manifests strong desires within. If a sense of privilege accompanies strong desires, then the person begins to fail in claiming accountability for his or her actions. Even when breaking laws of the holy word, a believer still stands strong in new vitality after baptism. However, they face the repercussion of not knowing what to do next when shot in the head by a fleeting bullet. After that lethal bullet, you still are standing in the alleyway where you were just murdered.

"Am I alive still?" you question in conscious recognition that reality continues to persist.

Unequipped with a comprehensive form of spiritual intelligence, you are limited by the mind you previously once equipped as a conscious tool. Now it is unconscious, splattered all over the concrete with no further utility of that brain. What have you taken with you into this non-physical state?

"Well fuck, I didn't even think the astral plane was – real..."

Yup, now you are a lower vibrational spirit-being that is incapable of visiting higher dimensions of mind because you never graced yourself with an intuitive intellect to speculate their existence.. What is alive? I feel as if we exist in both states of dead-alive. Inhabiting parallel universes as two beings: one conscious and one unconscious.

We are spirits of the dead, as the dead are alive in spirit. The conscious versus unconscious relationship between the physical reality and the unrevealed mind is a relationship between parallel dimensions in currently immeasurable form. Why are physicists having a difficult time understanding the big picture of their discoveries? I think it is because there is an element of mind involved. We need to better understand our brains if we were to choose to understand what it perceives. We already know through quantum physics that the act of observation varies the outcome of what we are observing.

There is a real connection between the individual (or perhaps singular) mind and the universal mind. The universal mind acts within a sublime nature to provide hints of its existence as a personified universe. It has been frequenting scientific journalism that the universe is a living simulation. Splendid, they are getting half the picture. The universe is intelligence that acts through natural and physical forces. It is however very handicapping to intuitive reasoning to make metaphorical associations between this living reality and our scientific fictions of technology and computer simulations.

The physical living reality is a simulation of active natural forces that are integral to the evolution of intelligence. It is the observation of these natural forces in the reproduction of a lasting reality that makes us believe we are living in an intelligent simulation. But let us stop the madness, as we are just living in an intelligent reality.

"There comes a time when the mind takes a
higher plane of knowledge but can never prove
how it got there."

Albert Einstein

Many people believe extraterrestrials are responsible for shaping geometries in the crops of corn, popularly known as crop circles. The ET beings shape this imagery for us to better understand the complicated nature of the universe. They allude to the complex geometries that control physics in mass manifestations. They know there exists a medium of communication between symbolism and intelligence, and it is invested in their efforts to help mankind evolve at a higher rate and capacity. If I were to involve my unsupported theories in this book, I might receive much criticism because I do not have an education relevant to these concepts. Though, I will offer some thoughts on the universe and dark matter. It is in a relationship with the physics of mass manifestations.

Dark matter is an alluring mystery to the greatest thinkers and astrophysicists in this world. Dark matter does not emit or absorb light, yet it causes gravitational lensing to occur in the perception between us and a galaxy we are attempting to view. We can see beyond dark matter as in through it, but we cannot identity what is truly is. We fail to record any radiation coming from the dark matter, so what is it? It is my feeling that it is the unmanifest, a conception contained in a sort of paradox. Dark matter exists in a state of conception before its creation. It has volume, takes up space and has a weak interaction with other dark matter. In a sense, it is physical as far as we can perceive without touching it ourselves. It holds a presence that is evidential by gravitational lensing. If dark matter is perceived in a way where light beyond it is warped when observed, it must hold clue on how we perceive matter.

Unmanifest? If you have not heard of this concept, I suggest you research it more on your own. The unmanifest is creation before its conception. It is understood in Jewish mysticism and is a vital mechanic within the Tree of Life. Keter, the highest Sephira, is the source of the unmanifest. It is the "air that cannot be held" it holds all the unthinkable which is simply all that has not been yet known. As it is unthinkable, it is also unknowable.

Perhaps dark matter is the shadow of something we have yet to know. As dark matter is a creation we cannot perceive, we glimpse into the reality that much can exist beyond our observation. Dark matter is a vacuum for intelligence, yet that intelligence is unmanifested. It is the phenomenon of the unimagined.

All that we may perceive in this universe is all that our mind is capable of perceiving. We will not perceive dark matter in its true state if it is unknown to the workings of our mind. It is vital we understand something else the Kabbalah communicates, the unmanifest is simultaneously manifested. It exists in both states of the expressed and unexpressed because time is not a barrier to creation.

We will find that dark matter generates matter. "Matter cannot be created nor destroyed" Between the two states of matter is a spectrum of nothingness to wholeness. Atoms are described to be the smaller building blocks of matter that break off into lighter elements until they reach a state where they no longer split. The state that is reached is like the fabric of space/time, the same as the strings of String Theory. That is the far-reaching conclusion of something forming into nothing. Dark matter is nothing forming into something. Matter has the illusion of being destroyed and dark matter has the illusion of being created. We observe dark matter as it holds together galaxies as if it is 'something', but remember, that it is created as nothing because it has not reached a state of becoming something.

The dimensions of time separate the parallel realities of space. It is upon the conception of these realities being impregnated by dimensions of time that we find ourselves caught in the moment of life as we have come to understand it in nature. The beginning and the end both connect within one singularity, from which an everlasting life-force originates like a wellspring. It is like the shape of a torus, and it is a great source of energy. Energy is recycled through transfigurations within the singularity at the speed of its increasing intelligence. It affects all surrounding existence and serves as the working algorithmic intelligence for the applied universe.

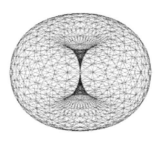

Vortex within a Torus
(the singularity is at the middle intersection)

The Nature of Keter is that something may appear from nothing. Ehyeh Asher Ehyeh is the associated godforce of Keter and it is also the name identified as God when appearing through the burning bush to Moses. From the inaction of a *part* of the bush, came the message of God through fire. At the mere coincidence of which you face divine intervention, God may appear from this *part* out of nowhere existing within Nature. Ein Sof is the divine source of light within us and is the source of the following Sephirot succeeding from its emanations. This source of light within the singularity illuminates our realms of existence. The graphic above shows a vortex within the torus. We can only imagine the potential energy within this intersection of two dimensions of time. The energy accumulated becomes a directive role and quality of Nature. If the operating intelligence of the singularity decides to create change within the surrounding matrix, it can do so rapidly.

Ehyeh Asher Ehyeh, the god-force within this singularity expressed itself by intervening with Nature. Through his sublime capabilities, God acted through the burning bush by creating a disturbance in physical reality to pass over a message to Moses. The intelligence of God is very acute; so, you find insight through him by very intense thinking. The capacity of the universe in intelligent design is so very complicated and advanced. We are far from the end of scientific progress, simply because we are approaching an irrational working of Nature as if it has a foundation in the rational. It does not. The rational has a foundation in the irrational workings of Nature. Scientific advances will eventually come off as incredibly metaphysical and phenomenal. Ehyeh Asher Ehyeh is a godforce from Keter, which means it is from the 'Crown' of intelligent Nature. It makes an intelligent intervention from the realm of Keter. Malkuth, the realm of creation or 'Kingdom' is the source of manifestation for humankind, animal-kind, and alien-kind. Binah as the sephirah of 'Understanding' is the source of consequential reality, simply because that creates understanding. Chokmah emanates 'Wisdom', which we gain from Nature. Meaningful moments bring wisdom and insight. Chokmah is a part of the meaning found within existence, accompanied by the understanding which follows it. The Supernal higher sephirot of Chokmah,

Binah, and Keter are all ways we are receiving the purpose of life.

The closer to Heaven you are, the more you begin to perceive everything with a seemingly irrational perspective that everything is connected and happening for a reason. This is the dimension of mind where God dwells, as he is a creation of our imagination. We are to follow the delusion, to leave behind the illusions of this world. The delusion provides an escape from physical reality. The separating distance between the rational and irrational continents of understanding and disbelief is the space between the self and the looming fog that enshrines the cognitively dissonant reality of Heaven. Death is a transitive process, a cycle of coming into awareness of a new existence, and it is through transcending this reality we come to teach ourselves about higher dimensions. The cycle of death and rebirth catalyzes the process in the development of consciousness. Essentially, through timelines and past lives, we are discovering the fifth dimension because, in awareness attention is paid towards the narration of such timelines.

God is of stories; he is found within the iterations of unfolding destiny as he serves as the head of discourse. The retraction of the ego causes the identity of self to dissolve into unspoken words. Those unspoken words are the framework of the unmanifest. Detaching socially ascribed secularistic beliefs from the foundations of reality causes life to shift into a dream. Within higher dimensions, we transcend and become sentient to dimensions higher than the physical matrix we are in. Higher dimensions work with universal mechanics that govern galactic bodies.

Practicing awareness, as a chapter, is about first making you cognizant of the parallel existence of other realities hidden behind the veil of death, which foreshadows spiritual liberation. I happily serve you with the conscious information you can utilize, to begin to explore altered states, sephirah. God's kingdom within your mind in the depths of your imagination, our imagination. The mind is cartography to the great architect in his pursuit to discover the greatest of all treasures. We are seekers to his discoveries within his divinity.

God becomes aware through our awakened states because that is when we relate to him instead of being a murmur that he does not see as sensible within his mind. In recollection, we are enduring within a dissonant reality under the Heavens. We have a demon and an angel on our shoulder, and we are lured with good and bad temptations. We align our will with the will of whatever god we worship through our actions. Now we must understand how to obtain the privilege to access a heavenly state of mind, which we do through learning and knowing how to get closer to God and the State of Mind where suffering desists.

CHAPTER FOUR

HEAVEN ON EARTH

The creation of Heaven on Earth will stem from the inspiration of an evolved perception of Nature. Divine inspiration comes out of nothing; it has no known meaning. It is every part of the collective participating in a mass delusion. That delusion is a near future that has deviated and evolved from present circumstances. Transcending the rational world forms the abstract foundations of uncreated reality. Heaven is an extension of that uncreated reality, as it is a formless inspiration, and inspiration is an indefinite source of the creative imagination.

The creative imagination is an expression of transcendental non-physical reality. We are locked into the left hemisphere of mind, which constructs reality based on absolutes developed through a revisionist rationality that suppresses creative nature. Within the right hemisphere of mind exists the indefinite source of human imagination. The emanations that are revealed from this source come from what I term as the Abyss. The traditional definition of the abyss is the portion of water beneath the surface, into the depths of the ocean where light cannot reach. In metaphor, the light of the sun is conscious awareness. It penetrates the surface of our conscious mind, and the awareness begins to dissipate at the point of subconsciousness. Much of our undiscovered imagination exist at the deepest levels of our consciousness.

I want you to understand that the intuitive intelligence I obtained in 2012 involved the concepts of higher self, the abyss, the void, etc. I learned what these things are within my mind through intuitive channels developed by my schizophrenic tendencies. I will continue explaining the abyss, but please know I am just now synthesizing my understanding of the abyss with its popular conception.

It is coincidental that my interpretation of the abyss and the one interpretation within the Kabbalah have remarkable similarities. Though it is not pure coincidence, as the source of the imagined Tree of Life is the same source I connected to in 2012. I will now conjoin the different interpretations and explain the whole picture.

Above the Abyss in the Tree of Life is the supernal triad of Keter, Binah, and Chokmah. In Jewish mysticism, it is believed that an individual cannot travel to the supernal dimensions of higher reality without passing and transcending the level of the Abyss. It takes dissolution of personal identity and a retraction of ego into being simply a conscious observer. You cannot traverse into ultimate reality, into higher domains of conscious awareness, without defeating costly deceptions of mundane reality. You will not have the capacity to investigate the higher divine if you are bound by your world of intellect and everyday experiences. When Mark passed through the Abyss, he entered a new reality of his own making.

"Abyss" echoed Mark's conscience while he was standing in his dorm room. The vehicle of his conscious awareness gravitated to higher domains of reality, creating a foundation where his perception and sixth sense extracted alternative meaning from within the context in everyday situations. Mark elevated his awareness into uncontained reality and began to hallucinate heavily. He began perceiving present moments of different realities across the fifth dimension of space/time as coalescing realities passing through each other in a massive reality constructed of Mark's perceived hallucinations.

With all the choices of realities to traverse to, the simple mechanic of the Merkava to travel into one of the higher realities was simply to choose to "believe" in that reality. Belief is a motivational force that surpasses barriers of logic, changing your conscious foundation into a new perception of reality.

The Merkava is the light vehicle of human consciousness; it is a multidimensional vehicle capable of moving conscious awareness through the different fourth-dimensional hallways of space/time. It traverses past fourth dimensional limitations by disengagement of physical reality. Disengage your senses from taught reality, retract your egoic identity, and become the status of a conscious observer.

Experience the transcendental reality of Heaven on Earth by elevating your psychospiritual disposition into an alternative headspace of belief in the higher State of Nature we know as Heaven. Move within your imagination, as your choice 'to believe' is the guiding wheel to turn into a parallel dimension of mind. Be prepared if you make this conscious effort. You will begin to hallucinate and surface irrational realities with delusion when engaging, as you explore higher realities of conscious imagination. I will meet you at the golden stairway, leading to the gateway of uncontained reality, the astral-physical environment of God.

Mark traversed different mental planes. Mental planes are uncontained realities of a different dimension. They are visited in mind, where awareness is a compass for the Merkava. The Abyss exists within the imagination, it is the essence of imagination where there is no existing status quo of world intellect. The Abyss leads into the Void and within the Void is a vortex of conception. Through exploration of these concepts, you begin to acknowledge the higher domains of absolute reality. Mental planes, which can be understood as psychological dispositions, are familiar to our psyche. Yet they are different to the physical engagements of this world, because as metaphysical realms, they function within the higher dimensions of mind. Mark can only explain it as being somewhere in your mind and seeing it within your reality.

The symbolic nature of language constructs hidden dimensions of mind to be interpreted by conscious awareness. Mark, in the middle of 2012, reflected on the languages of ancient civilizations. The alphabets of those past generations emphasized the gateway between reading language and the symbolism constructed within the mind. It intrigued him that language consisted of an alphabet of symbols and that the two-dimensional shapes could communicate realities in detail.

Symbols hold significant importance of their own, representing abstract ideas or concepts through attached meaning. Associating the cognition of mind with the identified realities is best done through symbolism, whether in language or art. We all hold subconscious information, which is interpreted and processed by the left and right hemisphere of the brain.

Science is performed through theory, mathematics, computing logic, and investigating natures of reality.

For something to be understood, it must hold relevance to the way the mind works. It works to rationalize unfiltered thoughts into a system of understanding and belief. The mind functions in accordance with a system of thinking.

The system of Kabbalah provides us with a complex system created from metaphysical realms, energies, universal functions into cartography, a map of hidden dimension expressed through the geometries and intersectional studies of the Tree of Life. Science is a process of understanding nature through real-world applications. Spirituality is the process of understanding nature through metaphysical applications.

Sociology of Religion helps us understand how we identified spirituality with the living experience. Totemism was the basis for this, as it was an early expression of us delving deeper into our imagination. Totems and objects were ascribed metaphysical properties, symbolic to the subconscious information we attached to them with spiritual significance. These items were ascribed characteristics that mimic the perceptions we encountered when realizing altered states of consciousness. Giving characteristics to items in symbolizing phenomenon was our first initial attempt to actualize a form of spirituality, to utilize the mind as a tool to project willpower and coordinate miracles with the relationship between the universe and Nature. How did an item of worship become a living reality for some of us?

We have adopted spiritualities from symbolisms and have journeyed into interpreting the creative hemisphere of the mind. We are endowed with a creative ability to shape the second-dimensional foundation of our living reality. Through the light within our mind, we envision a depth of meaning that is intrinsic to Nature. This vision is perceiving the holy emanations of the living order and the harmony of the absolute.

We are free to shape our collective social reality, through shaping our perception as living participants of our State of Nature. We are a glimpse away from a global awakening, which leads us to discover Heaven on Earth. The pseudointellectual practices you choose to guide your spirit into the higher domains of conscious reality is all in the result of your own free will and interpretation. Altered states of consciousness are not easy to achieve, especially in extremes. The spirit, belief, and aspirations of Heaven are dying off because of the parasitic nature of the rational mind. Our egos exhaust the spirit very quickly by challenging its very nature.

Misconceptions of God arise from the dissonance between Heaven and Earth. There is not a bridge completed, so we do not see God. Instead, we see the illusion of God. The differing temperaments of groupmind manifest multiple discourses of ethics and morality. This dissonance subjects our social reality to a median between Hell and Heaven. We are presently locked into a perpetual cycle of suffering as we are oppressed into obedience by the social structures we create, which obstruct personal development. We are engaged in a reality that serves as a precursor to higher dimensions.

It all began with the 'state of mind' concept, which was how I felt in the moment and where my mind was at. Mark experienced a state of mind where everything imaginable just, seemed completely possible. When you have ascended the stairway into Heaven which does begin at the footsteps of this world, you shed light into the unseen worlds that linger in foreign realities. This reality is the result of your intellect processing this world within your senses. The entrance to Heaven exists at the decision to see further, rather than retain life at face-value.

Attach your attention to the details of your everyday life. Decipher the subliminal hints that create a broad contrast between this world and a world of higher reality and perfect vision. Knowledge is presented up this stairway, with each step relative to being higher or lower in perspective. Making increasing sense is a forward process. Mark was baffled by Heaven, yet it continues to exist within him. Inside your mind, is a parallel universe a reflection of all that you have perceived within your life. It is your duty to question the vague realities that exist within and to determine what parallels you draw from them.

In Gnosticism, Sophia is the personified being of "wisdom" when referenced in the Hebrew Bible. Her presence in the religious text has diminished over time as the text has been tirelessly translated. Wisdom is "Sophia" in the Hebrew Bible, because of the context of which the word 'wisdom' is used. In Ecclesiasticus, she introduces herself to Earth as her exalted form saying,

"I came out of the mouth of the Most High and covered the Earth like a cloud. I dwelt in high places, and my throne is a cloudy pillar."

Wisdom is an attribute hidden away within the higher consciousness of this created realm on Earth. Sophia reigns over the Heavens of Earth, her face wrapped within the contours of clouds that show shadow where we are unconscious of her supernal being. In Gnosticism, is the belief that Sophia takes part in the creation of the Demiurge by carefully exerting her creative influence into the demiurgic matrix. Through acts of Nature, wisdom teaches us the art of perceiving the depth of knowledge concealed within creation. With wisdom, our souls can be guided from our deep slumber to awaken to higher realities only understood by the pursuit of increased knowledge. Knowledge is the salvation that frees the spirit and disengages the psyche from the realm of chaos.

At the middle of the night, we gain lucidity in our awareness and fly upwards to transcended reality. Have you noticed that you do not hold identity that is typical of the ego in your waking-state consciousness when you are asleep in dreams? Enjoying reality in high regard for what is amazing and profound illuminates a stairway of transcendence for you to travel.

With every step up the stairway, we conquer costly deceptions of the demiurgic illusion that entrap the spirit within an egoic identity. Upon defeating these costly deceptions, we venture further into the light. This light leads to the Ein Sof Ohr, a calling light that emanates from the higher echelons of Heaven. At the summit of the stairway are the heavenly gates, you stand there as your worldly self gazes over the symbolic gates of perception. As you walk past the gates, you are given a new higher identity; you experience your higher self. Gateways are symbolic in the mind. Egyptians raised pillars to represent portals to non-physical planes. To enter the gateway is to entertain the concept of entering a new state of mind, a new reality to be perceived with an altered consciousness.

Upon making a pact agreement of peace and harmony with Nature, it will bear the responsibility to begin to show you its true form. The spirits are often called to Sophia for her to impart to them her wisdom. Sophia illuminates our lesser self, so that we may find ourselves in higher forms of consciousness. Attaining the higher consciousness of self is extremely sobering to what is to be painted onto the canvas of our existence. When we visit Heaven, we are simply recollecting an independent source from which we were created. Heaven embodies different aspects of Nature through divine intervention, for calling ourselves to experience higher reality to identify with the source that birthed our spirits, the Light. Life is the story of self for the self to be rediscovered. Life is narrated by the liberty of wisdom, and the story is written in understanding through the power of knowledge.

In observing the Nature of this reality, you may encounter wisdom within the mind. Your mind may be speculating and conclude something making you simply wiser. It is because as Sophia is a shade of color within Nature, so is wisdom a part of observation. With good perception, you can see how wisdom is intrinsic to the creation of Nature as Sophia allows us to be aware of her presence. Taking on a new perspective is crucial to your development. Detach from your padded room of contained logic in new faith that all will be there when you return to reality.

Free yourself and spend your life living in the form of a fantasy, something other than the typical status quo. Happily, embrace being different and stop identifying with all the *sanity,* as who are *they* to tell you what to believe, think, and do? You came into this life to exercise your willpower. The other side of Nature is a real side of life. It is a whole other side of life, waiting to be lived and inviting you in with allure. It is crucial to embrace the key essential of 'a state of mind' when exploring these altered states of perception. This may be completely alien to what you have regarded as the concept of a state of mind. It is just an idea for now, until you begin feeling yourself make a conscious shift, which I hope you do.

Mark touches back to reality pretty much all the time. It is forced on him, like the rest of the world. Constantly trapped by everyday concerns, worries, and frustrations, Mark would admit that it is always hard to think about anything other than the sometimes-shitty life we are in. That sounds negative, but I am referring to this rut of a life that consumes all spirit, hopes, and dreams. If you have been curious to try psychedelics, you would have noticed that social barriers are easily detached from the ego as the identity of yourself. Magic mushrooms are wise teachers that provoke chemistry within you to perceive the underlying fabric of reality and the intelligent beauty within.

Under such an influence, one begins to perceive the universe with perfect vision. The mind notices patterns in life and creation because of no longer being jailed within the confines of this worldly matrix on Earth. Freeing the spirit takes you to higher planes of dimension where everything tends to gain meaning. You learn not to contain your spirit in a sad and limited mind. When you know you have nothing within, concern yourself with everything outside. When you no longer live in 'a box' that is paradoxically contained within a social environment, you transcend the rudimentary nature of everyday life. That is, you are no longer limited by the government and no longer limited by partial perspectives. You no longer fight with the reasoning of some perverted ideology you were educated on. You stop resisting and nod your head, only to turn away.

The spirit is the conscious awareness. The Merkava is the multidimensional vehicle of the spirit. Practice mobilizing spirit into the ascension of self into higher planes and realms that are not contained within social realities. I will shape a direction for your mind in discovering evidence of Heaven within Nature. We learn through visions that the 3D contained life we are familiar with is simply an illusion blurring a distant and higher reality.

The highest reality is that of the wholeness within the essence of creation, known as either the Pleroma in Gnosticism or the Ayn Sof Ohr in Kabbalah. We can also choose to understand this as 'Source', as it is the source of created imagination. As it is the source of all created things, it exists as a singularity, a wellspring flowing with creation. In Neoplatonism, we can better understand this concept. The Primal Beauty as thought of by Plato is the source of all beauty. It may be compared to the sephirah Tiphareth. The origination of all things that are designed with beauty gathers sourced energy from Tiphareth or Primal Beauty. In Neoplatonism, the soul is to journey in retreat to the Primal Beauty.

We have understood Atziluth to an extent, but it will serve us more if we continue to understand it as a world of Emanations. It is pertinent to begin to fully perceive what an emanation is in Nature. When defined, it is an abstract but perceptible thing that originates from a source. For example, when looking at a flower, you get a sense of beauty. That is because it emanates beauty. In contrast with another example, the emanation of wisdom can be perceived when understanding the insightful messages taken from the context of a situation or observation. Both are mind-compelling forces found within Nature that direct us further towards the origins of higher divine Nature.

When we introspectively ponder on why something is beautiful, we conclude that it is simply evidence of the cosmic harmony and higher reality. We are drawn to the Absolute. The soul in Neoplatonism is fragmented consciousness, as it was once part of the whole of Primal Beauty. The initiative is within the initiate to return to the source of these emanations through the psychic jumps of mind in evasion of this chaotic reality.

The Divine Absolute reality is a source of infinite pleasure, beauty, wisdom, understanding, etc. It is beyond all thought and matter and exists as an immersive spiritual experience. It is your choice to perceive the inner beauty of the moment and present, as existing within the emanations of reality is information which embodies a presence of foreign reality. Familiar with the origins of each soul, these higher realities exist as standalone metaphysical realms of thought. Realms of information are visited by the psyche in the mental plane. In each realm, are the different sources of archetypal realities, the descriptive emanations of reality (wisdom, mercy, strength, etc.) and these are part of the Kabbalist science of perceiving reality.

We intercept the light of Ohr by perceiving life in the *luminiferous aether* present within Ayn Sof Ohr, which illuminates each archetypal reality. The utility of a sixth sense notices these emanations of finer reality. I can best describe the sixth sense as a sense of knowing, as it is a cumulation of perception, awareness, memory, wisdom, and understanding. Through Ohr, a godforce is responsible for creating every dimension and part of reality.

As discussed before, the Four Worlds in Kabbalah are Atziluth, Briah, Yetzirah, and Assiah. These four worlds or domains within reality, generate content within creation that express absolute reality. From perceiving emanations of reality, we gain wisdom from where there lies hidden content. The four worlds are associated with the levels from the bottom of the Tree of Life to its top. Atziluth contains the emanating higher realities in Keter, Chokmah, and Binah. Briah is the perceiving realities of Gevurah, Chesed, and Tiphareth. Yetzirah is full of the physical and non-physical constructs of reality in the sephirot of Hod, Netzach, and Yesod. Assiah is the acting forces of creation in Malkuth.

Atziluth is *creatio ex nihilo*, which reads as creation out of nothing. It is an expressive force from the higher creative divine. Atziluth, the world of Emanations or Archetypes, exists as an abstract concept originating from the source of divinity. If you close your eyes tightly, eventually out of nothing light is found within your mind's eye and slowly expresses color. Atziluth is of similar conception, it exists from a source but is uncreated and formless. From the substance of *ex nihilo fit* … out of nothing comes something – which develops from the second world Briah, the world of Creation. It is simply a presence of unexpressed intelligence with self-awareness. It exists within the divine mind and holds territory, yet it exists without form.

This leads into the third world, Yetzirah, the world of Formation. Yetzirah is the formation of higher and lower dimensions. Things of nature are developed within a process of gestation, which awaits as a precursor to material manifestation. Assiah is the fourth world of Action, where an idea or concept is delivered into action as a force within physical reality. For example, it is the point at which an author introduces a character into a plot, whereas before, the character only existed in the imagination of the author. Assiah is where animation creates physical processes and things come into a complete manifestation of reality. The Four Worlds operate as microcosmic systems in which each sephirah offers a dimension to reality. Identifying the associated godforce and complex of the psyche with each sephirah will help you channel the inner light of Ohr. Channeling is an ability to probe the inner mind to mine intelligence from the collective groupmind. It is the result of creating a connection and becoming consciously aware of that connection in a way for it to surface within your cognitive capacity.

Now that we have understood the Four Worlds of manifestation, we will look individually at each of the sephirot within the Kabbalah Tree of Life. The higher domain of reality extending beyond the Abyss consists of Keter (crown), Binah (understanding), and Chokmah (wisdom), which are a part of the Supernal realities. In my understanding and interpretation, the Abyss is an inner dimension where feral spirits of the collective imagination exist. You could be standing in the middle of a grocery store and be plunged into the abyss, and upon entering you notice everyone around you had bright colored eyes leaving trails, and you see menacing spirits possessing their vessels. It is an altered state of perception; it is the haunting depths of your imagination. A lot of magicians venture through this dimension to practice the occult. To quote Gershom Scholem, he explains,

"It is the abyss which becomes visible in the gaps of existence ... in every transformation of reality, in every change of room, or every time the status of a thing is altered, the abyss of nothing is crossed and for a fleeting mystical moment becomes visible."

Scholem explains the experience of the Abyss very well. I relate to it, and I cannot compete. The Abyss is nearly unknowable; therefore, it is extremely vague in interpretation. I will emphasize two things, 1) the abyss becomes visible in the gaps of existence and 2) it is within a fleeting mystical moment when it becomes perceivable.

The sephirot of Binah, Gevurah, and Hod are situated upon the Pillar of Severity. They communicate within our realities a sense of justice, punishment, and purification, as well as the strength of glory for those who survive. The sephirot of Chokmah, Chesed, and Netzach are upon the Pillar of Mercy, the blessings of life hidden away from the world and higher reality. Let us further understand the Supernal Triad of Keter, Binah, and Chokmah. The highest sephirah is Keter; it is the sephirah that is a source of the Ayn Sof Ohr.

In the first world of Atziluth are emanating realities of Keter, Chokmah, and Binah. Keter is ascribed with the meaning of "crown" which can be taken a few different ways. As it is unmanifest, it is also the source of the created imagination which holds all that is intelligible to the Absolute nature of all things. In our psyche, Keter expresses the "is there, or is there not" part of perception, which is the sense of presence. As a realm of mind, it may be intellect as formed of nothing. Keter is the apex of transcendental consciousness and union, as it is within the boundaries of the Almighty. In Chokmah, wisdom emanates through the reasoning behind creation, as a sort of information bonded to Nature and situations with Nature. Through questioning of the very nature of something, you can perceive wisdom from appealing to direct insight.

Wisdom exists all around us from within the same microcosm where beauty originates. In Binah, a lot of lessons are taught for us in understanding. Many social situations are shaped by Binah to create a level of understanding to be learned. Binah brings meaning to the consequential nature of things in a world of action. The intelligible forethought of a situation that you realize in understanding is the emanating quality of Binah. This intelligence is communicated through the third eye. As mentioned previously, the third eye is responsible for processing emanations of reality.

In the second world of Briah, we experience the inner depth of creative imagination. Descending through the pathways of the divine into the Abyss, we find the three sephirot of Gevurah, Tiphareth, and Chesed. As the abyss represents the "gaps of existence" … it also represents the portals of mind into perceiving the Supernal higher realities. These portals or 'rips' within the fabric of spacetime tell us of existence beyond ours. Gevurah emanates the duality of darkness; it is situated upon the Pillar of Severity. Chesed is the duality of the light, as it is founded upon the Pillar of Mercy.

There is the strength and mercy of God, invested in the creation of our universe. Through Gevurah is the karmic force of punishment in the consequential universe. It is the unrelenting will of God to retain a neutral and meaningful universe, and he executes his will by both punishment and blessings. Gevurah is an underlying quality in Nature, that is a merciless force which combats wickedness and impurity. This creative Nature of the natural world commands Nature to call judgment in accountability for forces within order.

If a force is acting out against nature, the emanation of Gevurah provides strength to the will of Nature to overcome any presented chaos to suppress it. In Chesed is the creative karmic quality of the universe that manifests miracles and blessings. In the context of life, it is the hidden narrative that provokes us to be merciful to things and each other. The force of mercy within the hidden world sometimes coordinates miraculous events, sparks compassion towards victims, and encourages us to relinquish hostility.

The converging point of Chesed, Gevurah, and Yesod is the sephirah Tiphareth. Tiphareth is the creative inner depth of reality that is a source of all things beautiful. All the creation of God is beautiful by Nature, involving all the realms of wisdom, learning, strength, and mercy. All the higher sephirah above Yesod converge together into Malkuth, the kingdom in which we reside as beings.

There is the Veil of Paroketh underneath the beauty of Tiphareth. The sephirot of Hod, Netzach and Yesod are on the side of perception of Malkuth. Behind the Veil are all the sephirot from Tiphareth and beyond in higher residing realms. The higher reality is consequently cloaked in concealment. Yesod, Hod, Netzach and Malkuth are what the unawakened men and women are capable of perceiving. They can only see the 'Glory' of Hod and 'Eternity' of Netzach. Of the third world level of Yetzirah known as the world of Formation, are both Hod and Netzach. If you have been able to piece together these realms into a meaning, you will see into a depth of insight. Of the visible universe, we can perceive the glorious and eternal universe coming together in formation. As Yetzirah is the process of formation, the eternal glory of manifested reality continues to develop. The universe will never be *completed* as an eternal creation in manifestation. We can understand this, once again through understanding the Nature of reality, for example, the archetypal source of plant vines. Vines continue to grow in length and spread invasively. The universe and vines do not cease in growing until energetically satisfied.

If you put the puzzle together, you will understand how we are perceiving the projection of the 'Glory' of God in the Universe and see how all things are eternal. In Hod we perceive the glory of ourselves in magnificence, as well as the sublime Nature of the Almighty. In Netzach, we gain dimensions of time in the Formation of Yetzirah. The Veil of Paroketh allows us to only see these few things, the rest of divine creation is hidden away from the mundane. In the fourth world of Assiah, the world of Action, is the collective Nature of what we are most familiar with. It is our comfortable stratosphere of captivity underneath the Heavens of Genesis. Malkuth is the 'Kingdom' and its emanation as physical reality of material and nonmaterial Nature.

Understanding these several sephirot and identifying the ways they associate gives purpose, ascribes meaning to life, and helps one to identify the heavenly nature of reality. Heavenly nature is the original State of Nature for all creation; it is the fundamental process of life undisturbed by any unbalanced force. Deep introspection and discovery of these hidden metaphysical realms of thought, allows us to gain a sense of Heaven. We all have once had this sense.

Life as a child has a perceived sense of innocence that is lost throughout time. Think of the difference between a lively moment you may have had and the present moment. What is different in perception, the difference in the psychological state of mind? Consider the orientation of psyche you have presently and in the past. Wisdom promotes epiphanies that progress soul development. Wisdom ages the spirit, which matures the soul as it matures the psyche of the individual. Knowing that the distance between mental realities is measured out by the reasoning of Nature, it can be understood that the wisdom of Nature brings a climax to life. It is the adventure to the summit of intelligence that is hidden within the beauty of Nature.

Allusions to a higher reality that hold foundation in being cognizant merely by the reasoning with the existence of beauty, wisdom, and understanding, creates vision for something more authentic than just this physical dimension. This allusion to higher transcendental reality suggests that our secular reality is an illusion. The order and harmony of Heaven hold dominion over the Tree of Life on Earth, as you can see the heavenly nature resonating within the fabric of intelligent reality.

You can perceive that Heaven is the source of our Earth dimension. Heaven is only accessible in the past and future creative sources of universal dimension, which is not possible to visit in the physical and present reality. This means only in eternity are linear boundaries of time broken, allowing us to access the past and future within the present moments, making Heaven accessible as a direction in time.

The first sephirah that we traverse to higher realms is ironically Netzach. As Netzach has the quality of 'eternity', it is also the perception of time. The first step in perceiving Heaven is to go through and beyond Netzach. Understand that within eternity there exists the rigid concept of Time. You must go beyond your mind regarding space/time and its metaphysics to discover beyond this dimension of reality.

The most presentable methodology for seeing contrast between physically barred reality and a transcended form of reality is beginning to consciously sleepwalk as the spirit is in slumber. Usher mobility into your intuitive autonomy and act upon the soul, the psyche binding heart, mind, and spirit. This is performed by holding heartfelt obligations to understand all aspects of reality. You differentiate this lower physical reality from the higher realities by the ascension of mind. You know you are getting results when you feel as if you are 'truly' seeing things as they are and seeing the real reason why they are. Knowledge is presented up this stairway, with each step relative to be higher or lower in perspective.

Making increasing sense is a forward process, gaining inertia, that is gained with driven meaning in life. When you are in knowledge of an idea or invention in its raw material of thought, you immediately glimpse what it will look like in its perfected form. Through intuition, you find ways for the perfection to present itself in the ways you invent the thought and outline its manifestation.

We know something is perfect when it is meaningful to Nature. It is reminiscent of the supreme divine reality that brings us closer to fully realizing all of what is contained in higher Nature. In knowing the universal idea of something, you know the boundaries of its potential becoming limited by the laws of your mind. Finding truth in your opinions and creating harmony out of any internal dysfunction is a way of processing the spirit in discovery of the true self.

As you gain insights and epiphanies, you will become sensible to what you can only feel as what you have known all along. Through engaging a state of mind, the mindset is an acting gateway of communication between the divine higher mind and our lesser mind. This gateway of connection processes all emanations of the natural divine and produces intelligible thought.

Visiting Heaven in mind is a learning process, it is a duration of processing the depths of inner meaning associated with every pattern in Nature. This inner path leads up to you as the centerfold of your existence. Seeing yourself in the order and harmony of Nature gives you a sense of belonging, and with that comes the responsibility for something you will know when you are aware. It is not our responsibility to become enlightened beings, as we can consciously choose bliss in ignorance. If being a sheep makes you happy, please continue.

For some, they accept responsibility. That responsibility leads you to the fulfillment of your destiny, as well as the arrival of enlightenment from the journey inwards. How precious, that undeniable desire to go further into knowledge brings us closer to the knowledge that relieves the stress of the unknown. The tension in not knowing the truth, and the rising anger from the expectations for knowledge to present itself, causes us to struggle in achieving contentment. Through acquiring enlightened perspectives and knowledge, we will find contentment.

The next world after this one is far different, far better. When our generations pass on to the next life, we will be greeted by the possibility. We advance. We go beyond. Some may find themselves repeating old behaviors. We are dissonant to a higher reality, that in which everything develops into an actualized state of perfection. We develop through reaching for absolute atonement in the creative struggle, to resolve every added measure of conflict. It is the sum of all; it is Heaven. Heaven as a structural feature of reality, is the essence of what we perceive as *purity* in everything as a natural form. My teachings have taken many turns through dogma and superstition, and, eventually, to the observable nature of things. Through my narrative, I have approached you with a phenomenon. You may now notice the intelligence residing in every act of nature, from that, begins your journey to perfection.

CHAPTER FIVE

TRANSCENDENCE

Walking from the known world into the absent Heaven is an entirely irrational ascent. You have no guidance for your intuition, as your gaze becomes dilated with possibility. The predictable becomes spontaneous so the instinctual mind is driven crazy. The scaling into Heaven has consequences for the unenlightened mind, as there is no definition for the purpose and a scarcity of reason. You will question every step, asking if it were the right one. This is to determine your loyalty to the spirit.

You need to be loyal to the unknown, knowing that every inspiration of action stem from a bottomless void. You will think to yourself, "I have gone crazy" and this is because you are competing between two very different worlds. You have fought forever for things to make sense, but Heaven was not intended in creation to make any sense.

It is an alluring unknown, calling on those lost and seeking refuge. A seemingly distant and obscure reality like Heaven is not created to give you meaning. It is created to dismantle all meaning in the universe because it is not a structurally rigid concept. It is open for interpretation and that is what makes it overwhelming. In Heaven, there is no control and there is complete freedom for expression. A glimpse into the light reveals everything is connected.

Higher dimensional realities are connected to this reality by thoughtforms. In traversing through thoughts and our mind, we probe the inner eye and see every thought manifested by imagination. Do not feel vulnerable being unable to know everything, because how would you know the irrational nature of Heaven exists within. It simply takes an imagination to be created.

The higher dimensional realities connected to us by thought persist within a vacuum of creation. It is undiscovered and unmanifested territory lurking within us. I will provide some entertaining content to you that may arouse your curiosity and excite your childlike spirit. The closest we can conceive to what a higher reality is in this universe is a lot like our experiences with lucid dreaming. Imagine an afterlife that is like our present reality but made of several million coalescing ethereal realms. The Merkava traverses into each realm by engaging beliefs, synchronizing, and entangling through altered perception. A Merkava "teleports" – it slips through one realm into another – simply transitioning and fading from one existence into another. These realms are subject to the process of gamification. They become like a game, with the mechanics of one, as well as the added creative touch of fantasy.

Our imaginations invested in the popular culture of different movies, video games, and storytelling games, all that has been written, drawn, or painted, or anything that has been conceived exists within its own bubble of conception within the Void which is the vacuum of space/time. It exists there independently, awaiting to be surfaced and investigated by a wandering creative mind. As an astral physical being existing in a dimension of space/time, you explore hidden realities and live upon worlds beyond your present imagination.

Feeling is an intuitive art form, and to feel is *to know* when learning your environment. Feeling encompasses the state of mind you are engaging by exciting the emotions to shape inner well-being. Your well-being is captive to the social environment we live in. We are individualized by increasing awareness and the subjective experiences we have personally. Through these experiences, we build a relationship to the scenario.

We feel a certain type of way about the engaged reality and behave in reaction to it. Feeling out the inner emotions and depth of Nature is dependent on how well you know the divine Absolute. What kind of relationship have you gained with your existence? We all hold strong sentiments towards the circumstances in which we live. Is this truly necessary? Passion does well with these sentiments because it offers a driving force to motivate us. History tends to repeat itself unless the cycle is to be broken.

Being quick to divide, judge, and separate, are the destructive tendencies we learn from what we have experienced. As a young soul of an earthly realm, we are quickly manhandled into a pit where we are forced to release any innate ability to think soundly regarding the inner self. We are tagged with patriarchal family names to be trained to fight and sacrifice our lives for the command of tyranny. The matrix we live in is reproduced through spoken words and actions. It is a matrix of collective intelligence that has been refined throughout human development.

Through practicing a connection with the universal divine, the apprentice conjures his spirit to emulate a god which desires him, but more importantly, one he identifies to be omniscient to this desire. It is through this knowing of himself through God the apprentice achieves a direct and mutual relationship with the divine. In a quick arrangement of mind and spirit, the body gives life to a new mind that links spirit with the simple knowledge of divine creative authority. After the apprentice reaches this point, he is a craftsman, and by his physiochemical reproductions of the material world through transfiguration brought on from the clarity of gnosis, he crafts the image of his God. He then becomes a journeyman, seeing his God through the inner works of the modern sphere of collective human consciousness. In his journey, a messenger of human contact gives him the subliminal detail of the great work surrounding the journeyman and his invested higher self to the era of his evolution.

You become a vessel to the God that operates within you. You are held to a privilege of free will, and your decisions alter the progression of actions you are set to fulfill. The wisdom of Sophia belongs to the higher divine. Therefore, wisdom leads you closer to understanding the boundaries between yourself and the higher divine, along with the understanding of what it takes to transcend such limitations. In the effort of transcending the daily struggles of life are the opportunities to yield more information from those challenges. While practicing awareness, you can develop a keen sense for the insight of higher intelligence. You become aware of the demiurgic illusions as scenarios are constructed for you to endeavor. Enlightenment is not simply attaining the understanding there are godlike forces at work, enlightenment is found through the contentment knowing your time can be spent in the very efforts to transcend mundane reality.

Theravada and Mahayana Buddhism have conflicting perspectives on enlightenment. Some argue that it is a lengthy process, whereas some believe it can be experienced in an instantaneous moment of realization and awakening. It is clear to me that both have an argument, so enlightenment must be the reality of realizing the enlightened state and the process of obtaining spiritual liberation. You may have gathered something by this point about the 'state of mind' concept. If you are not sure, let me tell you what I have learned that led me to write this book.

Heaven and Hell are both a state of mind.

In 2012, Mark had the overwhelming feeling that anything could happen. When his altered state of mind was positive, nature was prettier, and the air was crisper. Everything within pleasure was magnified, and Mark could not get enough of it. Now that Mark is just a shadow of my inner identity due to continuing to take antipsychotic medication, I cannot help but remember what life was like in 2012. I cannot express how much I want to go back to these altered states of conscious reality. God was real and angels were all around me.

I even witnessed the love of God, as there were moments in which I felt like I was being loved even when nobody was around me. It was like how oxytocin is released when being hugged and comforted, except nobody was there to hug me. I was simply wrapped up in the caring love of the higher divine. They say God's love is everlasting. I can assure you that the kind of love I received from the dimensions of higher mind and heart could be sufficient in serving me for an eternity. All that is different from now compared to back then, is now I can choose to be ignorant of those experiences. Though, the difference between higher and lower planes of mind is distinguished by the type of state of mind that you have.

Heaven is a STATE OF MIND. Hell is a STATE OF MIND. Your ETERNITY is within the confines OF THIS MIND. Alter this STATE and go BEYOND MIND into SPIRIT.

If you wish to achieve great status, you must choose to embark on the greatest path you have found. At the defeat of existential reasoning and finding there is no simple purpose to life, you realize there is no evidence of one. This is because purpose and manifest destiny are each birthed from within the womb of the spirit. Human inspirations stem from finding potential solutions to a unified purpose. Inductively thinking in a manner that allows the emotions to feel heightened in aspirations that are achievable when considering many different possibilities. These circumstances that we dream of, provide a figurative outline for how we structure a foundation within our aspiring self. Motivating inspirations within for engaging new psychological dispositions allows yourself to go deeper into the Abyss, deeper within the rabbit hole. With endurance, a spirit can progress deep into the Abyss and illuminate the unconscious mind. Look at how you consciously perceive reality, as within the capaci-

ty of perception you may mine the universally embedded intelligence of source energy.

To exposit information from universal intelligence,
otherwise known as the divine mind, you must be accountable for your methods. First, the information you
may be gathering may be rather vague and incon-
sistent. Illuminate the process by cycling information
from within your mind. Use dualistic concepts as a
framework to further refine what initially starts off as
a bunch of thoughts and ideas. Consider the duality
between light and dark, masculine and feminine,
knowledge and wisdom, introversion, and extrover-
sion, etc.

Let the light that illuminates information pass
through each of the sephirot, creating a connection
from lower reality to the higher divine reality. You
would be a fool to assume there is no critical thinking
involved with any of these techniques. You must use
your ability in reasoning to touch upon something reasonable that may be justified by other things you
discover.

Faith is a lower form of awareness; it is simply the
wisdom without the knowledge. It is not lesser than
simply knowing, though it is an absence of
knowledge. Intelligent knowledge is to be discovered,
which is contained from your consideration by only
the limits and potentials of your faith. Faith is subser-
vient to theoretical rationality simply because it

prevents the mind from being chained by barriers that are constructed in concern of feasibility.

When faith evolves into knowledge, you gain self-esteem within your soul. At the higher end of conscious awareness is the communion with the divine. In this state of mind, you are familiar with intelligent Nature presenting itself in physical dimension. You recognize patterns, interpret lessons, find the truth, and learn that truth is all harmonious within Nature. Position wisdom and understanding onto pillars. Those pillars will serve to represent a portal to an altered state of consciousness, creating a gateway to traverse through when communicating with God.

The two pillars deliver a standard for emerging thoughts from Da'at (knowledge) to meet the ideals of brilliance. If you hold predispositions to expect the truth, then the truth will come from within the depths of your mind. Divine inner truths are balanced, even when confronted with the accusation of being blasphemous. Divine information is defined by divinity because it holds essential irrefutable truth. Muster up a few curiosities of your own and develop a practice of self-constructed methodologies to probe your inner self that is in connection to the divine mind. With your curious nature at heart, enter a trance in which you take the curiosity and draw information from within. Take on altered states of mind to reflect intensively, and further refine the curiosity into something you may have an answer for.

The purpose intrinsic to our capacity for developing informative insights through reflection and introspection is that we were created to advance further as intelligent and spiritual beings. We are to actively pursue the mission of becoming active participants in God's creation of the Universe. Like the Creator God, we are also creators in development.

The fully unlocked potential of our consciousness will allow us to manifest the non-physical interiors of mental dimension into the physical. From orchestrating higher dimensions into alignment, we construct dimensions for the concepts lurking in our mind. This is the great extent of the human capacity for intellect. What may not be achieved at this very moment could be achieved by the moment of realizing how to bring an achievement into action. In the chance of future conscious evolution, much of this may be possible.

The faith of which my thoughts appeal to is not of blind faith. Much of the content in this book may be understood. Though, what has been written only reflects the current situation of the present State of Nature we exist in. You may be merging into higher reality for the first time, or you may have been transitioning for a period now. Having a relationship with divine Nature allows you to see into the current predicament of reality.

Obtaining the insight of what creates chaos in this material dimension reveals to you why much of finer reality is undiscovered. We are often ignorant of anything that proves our constructed beliefs to be wrong. The meaning of life sustains youth and delivers cause to an eternal universe. The revelation of meaning within Nature puts an individual into an enlightened state of awareness, which affects their behavior by giving an added sense of character and role. Your connection to the meaning of life is the fundamental change in redefining your life.

Act out yourself through your willpower in harmony with the forces of nature to shape Nature in a way it revolves around the discovery of yourself. In manipulating the cosmic drama to be about you as a participant, you find allusions to your higher self within the subliminal nature of life. That meaning transforms the sum of you as a being and reveals the destination of yourself as a potential higher self. Within the narrative and knowing, you recognize your greater potential. There are fundamental dimensions within reality that are comprised of your reflection upon the natural world which encompasses all projections of your higher consciousness.

This dimension of the natural world lacks definition for your mind to develop consciousness in relationship with the external world. Investigating this dimension is a process of becoming one with Nature and higher consciousness. You find an aspect, a spirit of life, and you discover the same spirit of omnipotent potential in every man because God created him in their image. Unconscious behavior is integrated into the unconscious mind. The more you continue to develop a subconsciousness within your psyche, the further you go in development of awakening the soul.

The soul can develop the kinesthetic nature to travel to cognitive realms of mind to interpret realities in different ways. Through exercising your willpower by interpreting the Nature of reality, you ultimately gain a sense of Heaven and what that truly means. You must consciously 'opt-in' to the divine inner programming of Nature before having any real sense of benefits. If you do not 'opt-in' consciously, you may read as many spiritual books as you want and still gain nothing. You are inescapably engaged in a physical reality governed by the forces of Nature; how could you not see God in the picture? The matrix is full of creative meaning; our influence is of social construction. A mode of life, also known as a religion, has the purpose of serving ourselves.

Eventually, you will fully understand that it requires a shift in perspective, as result of growing theory, to fully embrace irrational realities. In practicing this state of mind concept, you must intuitively counter the implications of time and impossibility.

The process of self-developing a psychic nature is essential for being capable to gravitate towards hidden insights of the unaware mind. Your ego is contained within what you define as your purpose, and your unawakened soul is held captive by a dominating ego. If you were to believe in a higher calling, then your soul has reason to awaken beyond the constructed social matrix of our worldly realm. You are held to the sephirah that you engage your senses in the most, and for many, that is the Assiah Gashmi of Malkuth which is traditionally understood as the physical world.

Within the nature of God are many plans orchestrated to be fulfilled at the will of an evolving universe. The schematics are present, and only we are to construct the image of what is represented. What is to be fulfilled? I suggest that it is the completion of ourselves. The universe is a sandbox for all projections of God. Mind you, we are projections of God as we are created in his image.

As we grow up and our souls ascend to higher and less limited perspectives on reality, we lose sight of a God that we claim has human characteristics. It may be argued that we only attributed him those characteristics because we are only infants ourselves looking for a familiar face to see. The creative nature of self is an allusion to the irrational self as a spiritual entity.

The closer we come to identifying God in creative nature, the closer we approach the irrational realities in which God as a being exists. The creative nature is exercised through writing, painting, music, etc. In creativity, we are working with an aestheticism that revolves around brilliance in its primal form. If you neglect the creative nature of self and discontinue your belief in the extent of your imagination, then you are fulfilling a discourse that leaves you deceived by the mind and expelled from the heart. The heart and parts of the mind are known to be irrational, why question that very nature?

What if God was held to silence when acknowledging whatever prayers have reached him? His imagined heart would probably shrink in despair at the onslaught of upsetting prayers and cries for help. Some empathy in his direction and you may consider that he wishes to act but come to understand that he just does not. In teaching us to be independent agents of free-will, God hopes we may learn the consequential nature of our intentions. Atheists argue that a loving parental God would serve his children and answer them directly, thus if he had not, then he has failed as a God.

This is a rather limited perspective on what it means to be God, as if we had any real idea. You could give your heart out to a silent God, but that would teach your heart to be silent, for your mind to understand the silence. That is what makes silence divine in Nature, in understanding, there are no words spoken. With a passion that resonates within Nature and unlimited emotions that are never contained, you may fuel your persistence to come to the destination of God. Some people consciously choose to escape God out of fear; therefore, they do not act upon his callings. Not acting grants an individual temporary satisfaction, allowing the security of not changing. You may deliver yourself from an unstable situation by acting, and ultimately, be rewarded with the satisfaction that you chose to act.

The irrational drive of mankind to act out against the threat of Nature is the sourced energy that comes from the spirit. It takes spirit to break from this contained reality of death and you will see that come true in your wish to flee from an endless slumber. As from that final break to everlasting rest, you will wish from fate a second chance. In a probabilistic universe based on chance, you will make another life, a living reality that is eternal, from the moment of losing sight of death through believing once again in life. Paralleling minds in a shapeshifting universe, conceiving of connection in which walled boundaries break and hearts conjoin to find harmony in the onslaught of unnecessary evil, to find one whole truth that is love.

It appears we all reflect each other in whatever perspective that may be, and we are all on the frontier of experiencing harmony. As an author, I am prancing around making presumably illogical statements in the chattering of your reading conscience, this is only for your heart to play with me until you feel satisfied.

CHAPTER SIX

ADDING PERSPECTIVE

What happens upon death? You enter the origination of yourself, the unmanifested singularity of consciousness. You enter a fixed state of conception, a dwelling of potential. Meaning is deconstructed, and death is consequently meaningless. You become victim to the climax of your imagination, which takes your formless spirit into a developing cocoon, and that cocoon is determined to be an evolved expression of your eternal essence. We slip into an unconscious transformation of the soul and end up being materialized dimensions of the void. A paradoxically evolved consciousness forms from the absence of existence, and like butterflies we are released as independent forces of Nature. We continue to fight for the unimaginable until everything collapses, and reality is reborn in a higher light. This is the point when we become conscious again in a new creation of our making. That world is further reaching than the horizon we are familiar with.

In accepting the given conditions of reality, you are accepting the mundane Nature of reality. To participate in the divine grand scheme, you must see that things come forth in their appropriate times and places. That means to not falter because of any disturbances caused by lesser reality and direct action into existence as preordained by the natural order. In facing the consequences, everything is skewed slightly into a perspective where you are held accountable for your suffering. Then, your actions are credited towards a universal reputation you hold among peers, if it suffers, you ultimately suffer. This is a feature of consequential reality which makes the demiurgic matrix perfect for the self-realization of spiritual beings. It is ideal for us to find and realize perfection out of what is flawed and unrefined. The flawed creator, the demiurge, has a relationship with the population of our world. The demiurge oversees the operations of the world and provides illusive limitations on our spiritual growth and ascension beyond the physical world. A purpose of spiritual growth is to experience union with higher reality.

The demiurgic matrix, otherwise known as the world system, is a part of the illusion that suppresses minds from entering absolute reality. The illusion is the thought that reality is separate from spirit. The demiurge alienates the psyche from the higher world of spirit by attempting to merge the egoic being with physical nature through the relationship of matter. By constantly identifying with material reality, the higher spiritual reality is rejected. Success in preventing the alienation of psyche from spirit, allowing one to experience the whole relationship between self and higher reality.

We all must find meaning if we were to grow beyond into something more than simply observers of our surroundings. To actively participate in directing your purpose, you must understand why it holds meaning. Life as we know it is full of endless suffering. To what blessing or reason that the suffering embraces in endless trial, we are only to speculate. The thought of destiny is not real to those who do not believe in it, as you will not have a destiny you would be aware of if you did not believe you had one. Without death, there is everlasting life and infinite possibilities without the fear of losing attention to detail. The great works of the spirit exist through the winds, vegetation, and creation.

Death is an individual experience, as nobody is aware of it when it occurs to the subjective mind. Death is the moment an intelligent life retracts into a preconceived state of awareness, a soul, as we are only aware that the idea lives on within a lost somebody. Underneath the veil of the physical and perceivable is a lower dimension where thoughts and ideas hold significance. A lost somebody is an unborn dream being manifested into a collective living reality.

We are in part of Nature, as our surroundings are ultimately constructed within our interior mind. Inside the mind of one passing into death, a shift of perception is born in which they peer into their mind to realize God is a part of themselves. Added significant realizations fuel higher-level consciousness so they become observers of their own internalized Hell or Heaven.

Physical perception, spoken words, and semantics define your barriers within a matrix constructed by physical meaning and absent of existential meaning. This cold and meaningless descriptive framework of reality is the flawed creation of the demiurge. Your intelligence works in opposition to the demiurge through finding universal meaning in the union experienced beyond the matrix. Your purpose found within this union is what redefines the human experience as the spiritual fulfillment of destiny.

God is the presence of the surrounding universe, and the demiurge is the presence of the world system. Each hold characteristics which shape the way we perceive them. In the Apocryphon of John, we learn that the Almighty reflected his image upon the face of Barbelo. Barbelo is the androgynous mother that is the womb of the visible universe. The dualities of masculine and feminine energy are birthed into a dimension of Nature through the Almighty interacting with Barbelo.

Intelligence is a vacuum, a void, to be thought of. Imagination is a bottomless pit of wonder, a creative abyss. The intelligent void and creative abyss are in equilibrium, so we have a capacity for conception. We are birthed by our imaginations from the forming of our intelligence. In the void is the source of unmanifested light, and in the abyss is limitless space. The Ayn Sof Ohr is a limitless and indefinite fullness of light. We stem from the Ayn Sof Ohr through the pathways of light within our neural networking. We receive constant stimulation from this intelligent light of Ohr, and it is why we can animate our bodies. It is also why we can perceive physics of the universe and correctly perceive what is essentially occurring in real-time.

We are all one with God. This is because God functions as an archetype within the psychological interiors of our mind. God as a working principle, and as a grand speculative deity of our mental architecture, is a part of us which relays emanations of supreme reality into living physical reality. God is a projection of our imagination, which creates a reference to higher reality for us to ponder and eventually discover. Each of us can recognize inner divine reality occurring within the world, though it is a subtle difference. God is the working principle of our unconscious realities. From the brief concept of an archetype, to creating the perception of such, then creating the formation of natural forces which bring together and infuse imaginative reality to matter. Natural forces act to form physical reality and give life. Then in the world of creation, development of spirit occurs, only then to materialize in the world of matter and physical dimension.

On the other hand, God as an indwelling archetype of our mind is an oppositional force that will never cease. What we must understand of eternity is that ideological warfare is everlasting and always present in lower dimensions. The mind of God that is the divine framework of this living universe is a host of all forces both good and evil.

The cause of the all-natural singularity is the effect of all intelligence. The all-natural singularity is an eternally present cosmic event that exists in the essence of space/time. The essence of space/time exists in the mind. Infinite intelligence is existing in a state of matter during conception. This source gives a human conception of the Big Bang theory, which delivers dimensions to the active intelligence of our creation. Nature is that intelligence in effect. The singularity is serving as an alpha and the polarizing singularity as the omega.

God is the force of Nature and the order within it is his kingdom. The forces of this Nature are godlike and can defeat any opposition that is encountered. The strength of Nature is a force of consequence that eliminates sin performing intellectual rebellion. To go against Nature by exerting your will would be to excite the forces of destruction, meeting the ends of all illogical sentiments that oppose the moral and ethical principles of the living God. To intellectually debate the forces of Nature is self-defeating because you cannot eliminate the divine by dividing the existence of Nature with intellectual willpower. The wonderful thing about Nature is that it holds a composition of truth and harmony found within the divine law. The divine law holds the quality of being true and is unlikely to conflict with anything else holding truth. Therefore, it holds irrefutable meaning.

We are within a continuum of time known as Samsara; the repeated opportunistic universe known to recreate itself. When a man dies, he is reincarnated in the next life. If mankind is wiped out, his history is recycled, and a new dimension of time sees that the human spirit survives through transcending past death. Samsara is a conditional matrix in which many variables hold influence on levels of both macrocosmic and microcosmic. Samsara as a conditional matrix resets an environment until circumstances are fit for the surviving evolution of intended creation.

In Gnosticism, it is acknowledged that the current physical realm we are captive to on Earth is within the realm of chaos. The realm of chaos is a haven for inferior minds, for hatred to be acted upon by misunderstandings. We enjoy inflicting pain on ourselves as we are the projections of our imprisoned mind. The spirit brings out the worst in people when it is mishandled. Free will exists beyond our imagination but within our feelings.

There existed a time in a previous something-universe when everything came together and functioned upon each other in the co-creation of harmony. That harmony created the conception of the heavens. It may be said that something came together to form the big bang. That history exists in a fixed state of conception in the outlying universe beyond boundary because it reflects an idealistic universe that is our present universe. The "something-universe" imagination I am attempting to project into your mind, is what formed you from stardust. Simply put, it is things coming together in harmony.

The creation of the Universe started with abstract concepts like infinity, eternity, foundation, etc. The formation began with an observation of Nature within the fully realized conception of the Big Bang. Upon the observation by Nature as a collective entity, the pooled imagination developed action of the manifestation and actualization of the Universe, as the environment was conceived from the surrounding awareness. Spirit is the structured atomical conception of evolving and animating physical matter. It fuels matter with an energetic nature. We are an expression of a Nature that identifies with itself. We are the reflective Nature of the Universe. The progressive willpower of predestination is created from the polarizing forces within dualistic reality.. This willpower is channeled from the intentions of light and dark, of Heaven and Hell.

I speculate that collective effervescence is what will save this world from its imminent defeat. There have been periods where it has occurred such as the Enlightenment and the Renaissance. Emile Durkheim recognized that within periods of civilization there occurred shifts in the human state of consciousness on a collective level. In metaphor, it is when the divine face of the universe makes a star a spectacle for us to enjoy as a pressure point for the crisis that fuels our existential desire. From chaos, we learn order, and it is through the existential crisis of mankind that we will all reach mass enlightenment by awakening through collective effervescence.

Go within the mind's eye and go far beyond this planet and contained reality. Actively forget all the taught base knowledge, to remember a Nature present before. Work to distance yourself many planes from this realm into the beyond, and ultimately receive presence and union with God. As Freemasons learn of the craft, us as non-freemasons learn a craft of our own making. In adding the perspective that Nature is fully related to the self, we are to act out against anything unnatural to the self. We argue with others over the very nature of the world and where it is to go.

Transcending is stopping the argument to teach of the present moment.

Living in the present moment, you have nowhere to go but to face yourself. It is a great project to figure out yourself, and as an individual being, you should only be concerned with yourself. Individual liberty is the original state of nature, that is, to practice your beliefs without worry of being declared heretical. This does mean that the Almighty does not mind if you step out of bounds if your boundaries are set within yourself so as not to affect others. Practicing spirituality has always been free of judgment without orientation to others but the self. It is something to be embraced.

If you made science into a religion of the natural universe, the god of that religion would likely be the variable that alters the following outcomes of science, which we know to be Nature. If you socially constructed Nature to have an intuition you would have a Creator being. That being would be the foundation of all known science, forming belief systems which evolve into religion.

As a schizophrenic, I have visited irrational realities. Schizophrenia in Greek etymology, means "split-brain" which could be interpreted as the rational and irrational brain being split, creating a dissonance to manifest within reality. I could easily go from making sense to not making sense when I am experiencing a schizophrenic episode. Often, I am fully aware that I do not make sense to the average individual. The roughest part of schizophrenia is communication. "How the fuck do I get this picture across to the reader?" mutters my mind when authoring this book, as the content it offers may be considered professionally (in the psychiatric community) as a disaster of illogical sentiments that is begging diagnosis and treatment. Hegemony in the psychiatric community seems to be concerned with 1) who can psychoanalyze the best? And 2) who can appear saner and more credible than anybody else?

People are very glued to the reality they are taught, and sometimes cannot handle much more than this reality without experiencing symptoms of mental illness. Mark has had connections with a few individuals, from good friends to his stepsister. These connections are best described as moments in which the other individual took a step away from rationality and began perceiving what Mark saw in his mind. These are beautiful occasions, to be able to dance with an imagination like there is no tomorrow. Through discovering the source of imagination, you make the conscious choice to fight off the fears that you hold against the truth. In journeying deep into the rabbit hole, you descend the steps into the abyss. The path is incomplete, and you lose footing, which causes you to fall deep, plummeting towards the bottom. You hit your head very hard once you hit rock bottom. You entirely lose consciousness...

Upon waking up, you notice you do not know how you got here. You forgot the fact you made this decision to be caught up in the darkness of space and time. Suffering from amnesia of the formal situation, you must communicate with your consciousness to find your way. Caught in your head, you only have yourself as the teacher, as nobody is there except in your imagination. You begin to perceive apparitions of past and future echoes, entities calling out your name as they perceive your presence. Are they from your past, or are they in your head? The solace found within the mind is enough to deprive sensory input and give causation to hallucinations.

Your inner voice echoes off the walls of your vacant and clueless mind. The atmospheric headspace confined within your consciousness receives the presence of all around your surroundings through echolocation. Your consciousness begins to perceive distortions of your inner voice. These distortions of the inner self seem to convince you that you are in contact with the dead. Now here you are, at the bottom of this hole with no sense of time or space, trapped in an ominous, and suffocating darkness. Your identity begins to dissolve, as you start forgetting who you are and your name. The brain damage must have been great when surviving that fall of consciousness. You swallow your self-pity and attempt to cope.

When your mind suffers amnesia, you forget your name and where you came from, so delusions begin to settle in. You start convincing yourself you came from here, this contained reality that you can only imagine as your home. A woman from above cries out in pain, causing you to recall having a mother, but you have no real concept of family. So, you can only describe that relationship as one of spirit. You become familiar with her cries of pain, but what do you know about pain? You are numb and comfortable in the darkness. You harbor the desire to investigate yourself. Yet, in admitting you know very little of yourself, you begin wailing your body in all directions. You're having a psychotic episode. Has it only been a few minutes since you fell into a coma? Hilarious, get ahold of yourself. God beckons with a laugh, but you do not perceive it.

You begin to arouse feeling making you incredibly maniacal. You possess the desire to crucify the voices that are mocking you from within. Those voices, rather distortions of your thoughts, start to fall away from their taunts and become friendly. Ah, you asserted yourself against the ego. God is impressed. Immediately you are caught up in a light of unreachable distance. The closer you get to the source of light, the farther you elevate from your sense of self. You begin to no longer care about who you are anymore. Upon not caring, you feel incredible euphoria. Was your descent of consciousness a mere death? Or was it an ascension from a nightmare into the subconscious nature of reality? The doctor says your name, and you quickly say "fuck". Your family grimaces at your profane language. You begin to recall how you wound up in the hospital.

We are spirits of the dead, as the dead are alive in spirit. The parallel nature of reality between life and death holds a separation in perception. The borders of life and death are settled in a momentary lapse out of Nature into a higher reality. Human nature is conditioned by sustaining the condition of the body, by giving into hunger, the need for nurturing, sleep, etc. The primal ego is innocent by nature, as it is the essence of self that heeds to desires which we are ultimately blameless for.

However, when the individual has characterized his nature with that of the material and not spirit, a depreciation of self-esteem in higher identity occurs. Temporary fulfillments of carnal desire render the higher esteem of self as weakened. The perpetuation of falling to desires that make an individual more comfortable in this lower dimension gives less comfort in the thought of leaving it to something more.

The call for divine intervention comes most abruptly at death because you surrender helplessly to the very force of Nature. The will of the universe declares you an inferior being upon death as you have not survived physical death. We are all valuable as minor forces in the universe, bringing both order and chaos which provokes increasing complexity to be solved by an infallible Nature.

The irrational drive of mankind to act out against the threat of Nature is the sourced energy that comes from the spirit. It takes spirit to break from this contained reality of death, and you will see that come true in your wish to flee from an endless slumber. As from that final break to everlasting rest, you will wish from fate a second chance. And in a probabilistic universe based on chance, you will make another life a living reality that is eternal, from the moment of losing sight of death through believing once again in life.

Life is a strain of existence in a retrospectively impossible universe. Which should mean if you were to take on answering life's biggest questions, you might always find yourself in some existential predicament fighting either against Nature or complimenting it. It takes fine willpower to compliment it because you concede your fallible nature and give your soul away to creative nature which speaks in absolutes and "does the math for you", in that you leave the proof to be resolved between those seeking proof and Nature. The proof is often not a concern for the intuitive occultist, as feeling "one with Nature" is more beneficial in applied metaphysics to the intuitive nature of 'feeling out' the Absolute. In claiming an intuition, you must be connected to extraordinary consciousness.

Alternatively, you may develop an intuition based on intellectual occultism which altogether becomes an informed practice of guesswork.

Through greeting all theory with a constructive framework of reasoning, your mind will be led towards analyzing the Nature of the divine. This may result in a glimpse of the Absolute. In that brief realization, you have found your rock of knowledge. Not many people seem to progressively seek forms of higher knowledge that altogether benefit their higher sensibility of self.

Few are egoic in their expressions of higher identity. Most often, this is because it is humbling and ego-dissolving to encounter the higher self. The higher self that is mentioned is the retrospective "you" that pardons itself into your conscience in moments to solicit new meaning into your life. The higher self, I found by means of my hallucinations and running mind. Mark would be sitting in the presence of a friend, holding two separate conversations with the friend. One conversation was directed with peering into the real-world perception of their brown eyes, but the other conversation directed into transcendent higher planes with shimmering light golden eyes: both eyes belonging to the same entity as the friend, but two sets of eyes denoting the existence of two selves in the one individual.

The higher self of the friend nearby, appointed golden eyes illuminated the inner conscious nature of themselves. The lesser self, the friend, simply looked confused at Mark with brown eyes. Mark is very used to seeing eye colors beyond the typical. In his imagination, they were allusions to higher identity in different realms of mind within sephirot in the Tree of Life.

The sephirah Malkuth is of the lesser dimension we understand as our present physical reality. Heaven translated to Hebrew is 'Shamayim' which means "elevations" or "heights". This ultimately means that we coexist with Earth in a lesser dimension, and Heaven is elevated in both distance (height) and dimension (elevation). Our higher self is a multidimensional projection channeled through spirit within the soul. As Heaven is of higher dimension, the higher self may only be projected through mental dimension from higher spiritual realities.

In the later year of 2014, my good friend was finding herself through spirituality and was reading through a book on spirit guides while sitting next to me in the passenger seat. She was reading to me and discussed how spirit guides worked in unseen dimensions. In 2013 when I received a formal diagnosis, spirituality was dead to me. I threw away the jargon offered by my imagination and declared it as foolish to go back. In the moment when she mentioned the existence of spirit guides, I was struck with emotion. I realized at that moment that New Age spirituality was more alive in wonder than I was, even though I had experienced what I had. My delusions were beliefs held by other people who were non-schizophrenics. The gift of clarity was bestowed upon me in learning that my passion for the immaterial universe was shared by so many other beautiful people.

The universe does not have boundaries because it loops unto itself perpetuating its existence, just like a planet in orbit will consistently follow the same path unless acted upon externally. The divine mind perpetuates the laws that govern physical sciences and is only affected by the consciousness that it has permitted within its acknowledgment. We are bonded to the Nature of reality, which expresses the necessary science to affect our inherent nature of being an observer. Nature changes you. It shapes you, unlike anything that yet exists.

Nature explores the intricacies of itself with stunning curiosity that catches our attention. Evolution of plant life, animal life, the universe, all is evolving intelligence. Instead of a dial tone as your internet processes, you get natural sciences progressing to outcomes. It is a working intelligence of a creator God or god force. It lives within us and takes us beyond rationality. A state of mind is a connection; it's applied philosophy. It is being aware and in control of the way you react to the opposing forces of reality. It is half-aware of everyday life and half-aware of what contains life within the meaning. It is knowing that every instance of time is within a continuum of unlimited possibility.

CHAPTER SEVEN

EPILOGUE

I live in a constant state of delusion. You call it Heaven; I call it reality. But it is still a State of Mind. When you realize Heaven is a state of mind, and the kingdom is within the heart you connect into a world of its own making. I live in an alternate headspace and every day I find reasons not to conform. Like the example of millions of people who form character based on their opinions of the world, I am not of this world; I do not live in a system. I am an effect upon this world. It cannot change who I am, it can only change my perspective and deepen it. I react with brilliance, and I know my only goal is to not repeat what others have done, but instead show them something different.

In my mind there are two paths: transcendence and ignorance. To transcend mundane reality, you escape the suffering and give it a new depth of meaning. You take on your challenges and frustrations, only to express fundamental change within the inner self. Keeping to your heart, you protect it with a willpower to disengage evil and to practice good works that nurture the soul with an expression of compassion. Remind yourself every day that you do have a heart and memories without love die off fast.

Reflecting on the first chapter, which described my first experience with psychotic states, I mentioned that I felt *biologically awakened*. Well, I truly was. Something within my biology awakened from a sleeping state, and I transformed with a new perception and came to new heights of consciousness. I do not look at life the same as when I was 18. Back then, everything was shallow and *just for fun*. Now everything has purpose, and my destiny is to enlighten. I can die happy now that I have made this book and my testimony available to the masses. I keep to the rhythm of my heart, as it beats with anticipation for a greater tomorrow. I know if I follow my heart, I will extend this present life into a new creation and a new world.

Mark is a shadow of myself, as he only appears in sight when the sun is at a certain point in the sky and the time is right. He remains mostly a mystery to me and has led me to face many crises of identity in the past several years. It was difficult to accept within myself that I am not the same person. I am extraterrestrial as we all are.

We extend as projections of life onto Earth from distant stars and galaxies. We continue to exist if there are living stars in the universe. That is millions, trillions, or more years that will pass until we have another slumber. Mark would tell you that this is the second chapter of Creation, and one unit of eternity has already passed. We will spend a *very* long time understanding the present unfolding chapter of creation. God is an author unlike any other. His writing and eternal inscriptions in the universe will offer infinite meaning and an infinite *sense* of significance. I do not think many people understand how phenomenal this universe *really* is. You will be content for an eternity upon these realizations. So just carry forward in your life and work to be humble and learn. You only have about 100 years on Earth, make it incredibly meaningful, begin living your testimony, and continue making history.

There are stars that belong to each of us in the universe. Revolving around each star are our individual solar systems. Eventually, we will create 'systems' that form the conditions for all galaxies we target. These 'systems' come from the second world of creation Briah. Simply, we discover these inner potentials within our creative imagination, whether it be technological or something beyond that from pure intelligence. A process of manifestation, otherwise termed as deliberate creation, is our responsibility in creating the physical dimension which in effect is constructing new realities. Liberation of flesh means becoming a being of observation. The principle of observation in quantum physics has a perceived relationship with an outcome of Nature.

Should I be stunned that I am finalizing this period of my life after all this time? Or am I simply beginning a new one? Much has occurred in my personal life since 2012 and that should keep me distracted. However, I wanted to express my '2012' to people. I have considerable desires that are acted upon an agenda of my own. It is my mission in life to help others become aware of this very complex reality we have found ourselves locked in. Ask my friends, they will tell you that I comment on how much I want people to see or know what I have become familiar with as otherworldly dimensions.

I feel like people must become increasingly aware of how beautiful and perfect they all are. Many people really *try* to succeed in living a good life. I love that people really exhaust themselves and continue to *try*. It is beautiful to me. I perceive a suppressed innocence in most people and learn to admire them for those traits.

The spirit we possess is a vehicle of the Four Worlds, used to travel between these worlds and deliver emanation, creation, formation, and action to the living construct of reality. We are entirely co-creators in a training process, learning how to develop obedience to the universe and deliver good works to Heaven. Agape is known as the love of God. It is a transcended form of love, as it is based on the love for human nature. Human nature is imperfect, so love it. Love others for the fact they 'try' their hardest and love them for their character. Blanket the whole of another with an immersive love and appreciation, comforting them on new levels. It is a love that people do not easily forget. It is a State of Mind.

How do you leverage belief in the personal imaginative realities you create? Well, it is like the 'red or blue pill' concept'; you either deny yourself as the keeper of your imagination and continue in belief of the social matrix, or you deny the demiurge as the controller of your imagination. To defeat the demiurgic illusion would be conquering all the sin, those lesser forms of deception that currently have our consciousness locked in lower developments.

My grandmother died during the period I have written this book. We were very close. She took very good care of me when I had schizophrenic episodes. It was normal for her to sit on the front porch with me while I talked to her and other beings and voices in my head. She was very intuitive and understood that I was gifted to perceive things beyond this world.

I told her things in 2012 that she held onto, because the words offered wisdom. Like my stepsister, my mental illness did not "freak out" either of them. My grandmother died in 2017 due to her health finally giving in after the many years she had with health issues. She remains as a significant part of my heart.

At the time of her passing, I was at a music festival with my good friends. My mother called me to let me know. I was shocked to hear from my mother that grandma had passed away that night. Though, my grieving process has not been typical. I never really cried much, nor did I get stuck in my bed.

The following summer I was working with my parents at their workplace, trying to make some extra income to support myself. I would listen to podcasts on Gnosticism, as that is what I identified with most at the time. One excerpt of one of the recordings discussed mourning the death of others. How as a Gnostic, mourning can be a little different and a little heartless. Of course, I miss my grandmother. Though, as much as I miss her, I have equal amounts of confidence she continues to persist. So, the pain and confidence equal each other, allowing me to continue just being.

Offered with the gnosis of insight through the communion of heart with the higher divine, I do not fear much about death at all. As the heart continues to feel for those lost, your heart continues to feel them as you are lost. As emotions are invested in the heart as a feature of our multidimensional soul, the memory acquainted with the spirit of higher consciousness continues to recognize the heart.

The psyche is bound to both emotional and spiritual intelligence. We develop a *sense* for the character of the ones we live beside. We continue to sense them as we pass into higher dimension. With all that I have helped you understand, you may comprehend the nature of this *sense* and how it may be compared to a sixth sense. It is a complex sense of memory and recognition, and it is partnered with your psyche. Those characteristic qualities of the psyche are joined by wisdom and understanding.

Wisdom and understanding are the results of conscious awareness and empathy. Empathy is the transferred emotional intelligence of the heart to the psyche. Conscious awareness is simply how many obstacles you have conquered when expanding your awareness and perception. So, the qualities of the sixth sense can be easily understood as the sum of knowledge. The sixth sense is a sense of knowing. When I tell you that through a channel between my third eye and higher divine has led me to know more, I am simply saying that I have gained knowledge through my connection with the higher divine.

Empower this sixth sense by understanding it and feeling it. How do you feel it? The same way you feel the feelings of other people, through the empathic entanglement of heart and mind with another. To sense for the higher divine and develop a channel, or a connection, you must feel the divine in its pervasive presence above our gaze. The providence of Nature and its connection to you is where you must lead your heart and psyche. Think of someone you love in a very genuine and unconditional manner. You know the love is true, heartfelt, and innocent by its Nature.

Innocence is characteristic to raw, heartfelt energy. Through your innocence, think of your favorite places around the world that you know and have visited. Imagine one that you have not visited in recent years. Do you feel a sense of connection?

Now, think of all the beauty in Nature. Think of how the air smells back home where you are from. It is within this perception that you understand Nature. And it is through this connection you have an empathetic connection with Nature. Now sum together all the feelings, understanding, connection, and express it as a raw imagination that will behave as a channel when you reference it in mind with your psychic ability. You will most likely have a channel with this part of Nature in which you can reflect upon. It will begin with curious questions as your mind wanders through all that you know by this connection. And it will end eventually with your mind sparking more questions into the unknown. As if there is a boundary between what you know and couldn't possibly know, break this boundary through empathy of Nature. What does Nature know? What does Nature feel? It is through this channel and skill that you will acquire insight.

The world will experience symptoms of confusion in their existence. This will fuel the coming period of intense self-realization in the masses. We are in the dark ages coming into another period of enlightenment, a collective effervescence. Every person will strain their minds harder than they ever have before, with an intensity of thinking that will give rise to an awakening. Every man and woman will transcend this chaotic world, and this is because God is *universalist*. This means that God will deliver every soul from Hell into Heaven, because his love will grow, and in effect his love will forgive each of us and offer an eternity to grow.

At the wave of the inferno, we all be set in our ways, and so it was then that we were cast into myths with only our hearts set in stone. The memory of us only grows fainter when we lose sight of all that we have witnessed. If we hold pride in a humble manner through keeping love at the center of our lessons, we will inspire the curious hearts who set eyes on our statues. Ages of civilization falter and eventually collapse but they continue further into the making of their history. What is left behind is a mark upon this world, and we are to do the same.

Remove words and understand everything. Then put the words back and understand more. When you shut your eyes, your mind takes over. When you open your eyes, your heart takes over. Keep yourself in a consistent state of reflection, and do not allow yourself to be weakened by fear. Much of this road is very difficult, but when meeting the end, you will witness the treasure invested within yourself which is the courage and stamina of your spirit. After defeating the hardest of challenges, your feet will gain traction in the desperation, and you will become a leader. I hope you begin to chart paths in the direction of the divine, because we as brothers and sisters will be framed within the hierarchies of the unconquered.

I wrote much of this book while experiencing hypomania. In those states of mind, I have a great capacity for creativity and embracing new and different perspectives. In the vision of Mark is a creative landscape full of symbolic features and indefinite meaning. Mark does not appear very often anymore. The antipsychotic medication that I take tends to completely block off those parts of my brain. My potential in enlightened states is a threat to the status quo, and so is anyone speaking differently. The only way to make change is to be the actor that goes off script and fills the audience with anxiety.

A state of mind is fundamental in accessing the *different* part of yourself that is suppressed inside. The solution to transcending the world is to no longer identify with the world, instead to alienate your sense of self from the chaos and reuniting with the collective identity of humanity that we each hold. In a massive shift of perspective in the perpetuating reality, we transcend the defeat of ourselves brought on by the world. Spend time with yourself and capture your own energy to begin to paint a picture of your inner world. Develop a relationship to this inner world and venture off within.

When adding perspective to your reality, you transcend limitations and begin perceiving Heaven with an acute awareness. The dominating rationale of this world that imprisons your mind will start to regress, and eventually you will find yourself seeking what is deep within the Abyss. In the end, we believed everything because we knew all along, that everything was possible. In that moment, we were enlightened. Good luck on your personal journey, friend, and keep yourself in mind as you venture off into this chaotic world, and eventually, into Heaven.

ABOUT THE AUTHOR

Dillon Jepsen was born in Bradenton, FL in the United
States in November 1992. He grew up in his
hometown during his entire life and went to college at
Florida State University where he received a Bachelor
of Science in Sociology. He developed schizoaffective
disorder at 19 years old, and after a year full of
episodic symptoms, he became an agnostic atheist.
After self-realization in 2014, he aspired to pass on his
knowledge. During his senior year at Florida State
University in 2016, he began compiling this book to
summarize some of what he felt was important
information to make public.

Printed in Great Britain
by Amazon

80202775R00086